D0526877

PENGUIN BOOKS

HINDUISM

Kshiti Mohan Sen was educated at the traditional Sanskrit schools of Banaras, which had been a centre of Indian learning for many centuries. He mastered Sanskrit and a large collection of modern Indian languages, and also became an expert on Indian religious texts at a comparatively young age. His interest soon shifted towards folk literature and rural culture. He walked many thousand miles through various parts of rural India, producing a remarkable collection of folk poetry and songs. The oral tradition has always been very strong in India, and Kshiti Mohan Sen provided a systematic collection of the works of bards of several centuries. He will be remembered particularly for his work on Kabir and Dadu, the medieval mystics, and that on the *Bauls* of Bengal. Along with his study of folk culture, Kshiti Mohan Sen continued his scholastic works on Hindu texts, and wrote several volumes on different aspects of Hinduism, including a treatise on the caste system, and a textual study of the position of women in ancient India.

Kshiti Mohan Sen joined the poet Rabindranath Tagore's efforts at building an international centre for learning and culture at Santiniketan towards the beginning of this century and stayed there until his death in March 1960. He played an extremely important part in the growth of the University.

HINDUISM

K. M. SEN

PENGUIN BOOKS

PENGUIN BOOKS

Published by the Penguin Group
Penguin Books Ltd, 27 Wrights Lane, London W8 5TZ, England
Penguin Books USA Inc., 375 Hudson Street, New York, New York 10014, USA
Penguin Books Australia Ltd, Ringwood, Victoria, Australia
Penguin Books Canada Ltd, 2801 John Street, Markham, Ontario, Canada L3R 1B4
Penguin Books (NZ) Ltd, 182–190 Wairau Road, Auckland 10, New Zealand

Penguin Books Ltd, Registered Offices: Harmondsworth, Middlesex, England

First published in Pelican Books 1961
Reprinted in Penguin Books 1991
1 3 5 7 9 10 8 6 4 2

Copyright © the Estate of K. M. Sen, 1961
All rights reserved

Printed in England by Clays Ltd, St Ives plc
Set in Monotype Baskerville

Except in the United States of America, this book is sold subject to the condition that it shall not, by way of trade or otherwise, be lent, re-sold, hired out, or otherwise circulated without the publisher's prior consent in any form of binding or cover other than that in which it is published and without a similar condition including this condition being imposed on the subsequent purchaser

Contents

Preface

UNLIKE other world religions such as Christianity, Islam, or Buddhism, Hinduism did not have any one founder. It grew gradually over a period of five thousand years absorbing and assimilating all the religious and cultural movements of India. Consequently, it does not have a Bible or a *Korān* or a *Dhammapadam* to which controversies can be referred for resolution. The *Vedas*, the *Upanishads*, the *Gītā*, the *Rāmāyaṇa*, the *Mahābhārata*, the *Purāṇas*, the books on the so-called 'Six Systems of Philosophy', the songs of the *Bhakti* movements and of the mystics are all authoritative, but none is exclusively so. The different schools of thought have differed on a number of important questions, and even today their differences are by no means insignificant. This makes the task of writing a popular book on Hinduism very difficult, for it is not easy to decide what relative importance to attach to the different schools of thought. I do not know whether the knowledgeable reader will find my interpretation of relative values acceptable. I have tried to be as impersonal as possible, but this is a field where personal bias is difficult to avoid. For some time past my criticism of many books on Hindu philosophy has been that they attach too little importance to the religious movements of the lower strata of society by concentrating on the documents of the more educated section of the people. In trying to incorporate the philosophies of the popular religious movements, I have attempted to provide what appears to me to be a wider view. I hope that most readers will find this presentation to be balanced, though I am well aware that this is a field where opinions cannot but differ.

I have addressed this book to readers without any previous knowledge of Hinduism. I have, therefore, tried to explain all concepts that may appear to the reader to be new. I have not attempted to make him an expert on Hinduism. There is a vast number of large volumes competently written on Hinduism, which the interested reader can easily look up. This book is meant as no more than an introduction, partly to give some basic ideas about the nature and function of Hinduism to people who know nothing about it, and partly to stimulate them to read more about it. I know that some readers will be disappointed by the limitations imposed on the scope of some of the chapters, for instance by the briefness of the chapter on 'The Six Systems of Philosophy', but that is entirely deliberate. I did not wish to add to the number of fat tomes on Hinduism and have tried to write something that can be read even by those with much else to do. The more scholarly reader must, I fear, seek satisfaction elsewhere, though he may perhaps use this as a first introduction, presenting, I hope, the basic features of most Hindu schools of thought.

I must give some explanation of the scheme of the book. In Part I, the nature and the ideas of the Hindu schools of thought are discussed. In Part II, the evolution of Hindu thought and practices is studied historically. And in Part III, I have presented a collection of extracts from various Hindu documents. The reader can, I hope, get some of the ideas first-hand through reading these extracts, which cover a fairly wide area.

Finally, I must acknowledge the help and assistance I have received from my friends and colleagues in writing this book. My education and background are almost completely Oriental and my thoughts find easier expression in Indian languages than in English. Almost all my works so far have been in Indian languages, and I would have had great difficulty in producing this book in English but for the help of my friends and well-wishers. They have also assisted me in various other ways in the writing of this book. I am particularly grateful to Dr Sisir Kumar Ghosh for his active help and cooperation. I have also received considerable assistance from my grandson Dr Amartya Kumar Sen in the presentation and arrangement of the book.

Santiniketan
January 1959

KSHITI MOHAN SEN

A Note on Pronunciation

DIACRITICAL marks have been used in the case of Indian words, including all proper names, except those belonging to the modern period for they are already written in a particular way in the European alphabet.

VOWELS

a as in America (the first a) or u in nut
ā as in father
i as in pin
ī as in police
u as in put
ū as in rule
ṛi as in rill (approximately)
e as in fête
ai as in aisle (approximately)
o as in so
au as in house (approximately)

CONSONANTS

Guttural	k	kh	g	gh	ṅ
Palatal	c	ch	j	jh	ñ
Retroflex	ṭ	ṭh	ḍ	ḍh	ṇ
Dental	t	th	d	dh	n
Labial	p	ph	b	bh	m
Semi-vowels	y	r	l	v	
Sibilants	s	as in sun,			
	ś	approximately like English sh; the latter is more cerebral, or retroflex			
Aspirate	h	representing both the ordinary aspirate as well as *visarga*, the strong aspirate			

Anusvāra	ṃ	pronounced in many different ways, but one of its main uses is to nasalize the preceding vowel.

Of the letters used without diacritical marks, it is particularly important to note that 'c' is to be pronounced not as it is usually pronounced in English, but like the palatal c in Italian (e.g. *cento*). Similarly t's and d's without diacritical marks are to be pronounced as in Italian (dental, rather than retroflex).

Part One

THE NATURE AND PRINCIPLES OF HINDUISM

CHAPTER I

Introduction

SOME four hundred years ago, there lived in India a poet-saint called Rajjab. When it was known that Rajjab had received his 'illumination', men from far and near came to him and asked: 'What is it that you see? What is it that you hear?' He answered: 'I see the eternal play of life. I hear heavenly voices singing, "Give form to the yet unformed, speak out and express."'

Life seeks for expression, it must speak out, as Rajjab put it. Man has to work and toil to satisfy his physical needs. But this is not enough for him; he wants something more, something which more than three thousand years ago the *Atharvaveda* praised in its hymn to Superfluity (*Ucchishṭa Sūkta*). First there is the feeling of wonder and awe at the mysteries of existence. In Hinduism, we find this in the Vedic *Saṃhitās*, composed mainly in the second millennium B.C. In the words of Rabindranath Tagore these were 'a poetic testament of a people's collective reaction to the wonder and awe of existence. A people of vigorous and unsophisticated imagination awakened at the very dawn of civilization to a sense of the inexhaustible mystery that is implicit in life.'[1] This leads to speculation, which in turn leads to theories of existence and life such as we find in the *Upanishads* (*c.* 800 B.C.) and in later Hindu philosophy.

This is one aspect of the Hindu religion. Another is its moral code of behaviour. Every religion tends to find a conflict between what men do and what, according to its values, men ought to do. This conflict is closely linked with man's concept of the nature of the universe. Once men are recognized to be the creation of the Supreme and all men are recognized to be brothers, the ideals of selfless service and sacrifice become obvious. Once the *Upanishads* reveal their

1. Foreword to *Hindu Scriptures*. Ed. Nicol Macnicol. Everyman's Library, 1938, pp. 148–9.

doctrine of the all-pervading God, the ideal of selfless work preached by the *Bhagavad-Gītā* is difficult to avoid.

We are living today in an age of science, and in many respects we are more fortunate than were our predecessors. It would be rash to say, however, that we feel more secure today than our ancestors did. It would be even more difficult to claim that our acquisitive society has achieved a harmony of individual and social living. Modern science and the social developments connected with it constitute a challenge as well as an opportunity. I do not claim that Hinduism has a complete answer to these perplexing problems of our age. But perhaps its basic beliefs and philosophy are not irrelevant to the problems of the modern world, and may perhaps help us to recognize the full significance of some of the questions that have been raised by the difficulties of this age. It is in this context that an account of the central tenets of Hinduism can be justified. In the past these tenets have influenced the thinking of nearly half the population of the world; partly through Hinduism itself, but also through its offshoots such as Jainism and Buddhism. That itself is perhaps a sufficient apology for writing this book. But it is the author's belief that Hindu philosophy, so far from being merely a matter of the past, has great relevance also to the problems of the present.

To explain the principles of Hinduism to people unfamiliar with its frame of reference is a difficult task. For one thing, some of the terms used do not have exact synonyms in the European languages. Almost every writer on Hinduism is forced to point out that *dharma* and religion are not the same thing; a *mandira* is not a Hindu church; *jāti* has been translated as caste, but it is an unhappy rendering. A word so important to Hindu philosophy as *sādhanā* has no equivalent in English. This is comparable with the difficulty in finding exact synonyms for such words and ideas as 'cross' and 'charity' in non-Christian cultures and languages.

The definition of Hinduism presents another difficulty. Hinduism is more like a tree that has *grown* gradually than like a building that has been *erected* by some great architect at some definite point in time. It contains within it, as we shall see, the influences of many cultures, and the body of Hindu thought thus offers as much variety as the Indian nation itself. It is not surprising, therefore, that A. C. Bouquet, writing on Comparative Religion, found that 'India in particular furnishes within its limits examples of every conceivable type of attempt at the solution of the religious problem'.[1] The cultures of the Dravidian and the non-Dravidian peoples before the so-called Aryan invasion, the actual Sanskritized Aryan culture, the culture of the later invaders, the influences of Buddhism, Jainism, and Sikhism (to which Hinduism gave birth) and of Islam and Christianity (which came from outside) can be traced at various stages of the evolution of Hindu thought.

This does not mean, as has sometimes been suggested, that the various branches of Hindu religion really have nothing in common. Doctrines have varied somewhat from school to school, but there is a certain basic unity among all these theories. Part of the reason why different answers have been given by different schools is that different questions have been asked. And even when the ideas have been genuinely different from one another, there has remained a certain unity of religious assumptions. This would explain why such apparently contradictory philosophies as the monism ('God alone is real') of Śaṃkara and the dualism ('When shall I be able to lay myself at Your feet?') of the *Bhakti* school have led to no violent conflict. Another source of unity is what some Indian philosophers called *caritra*, conduct or character. Provided there was a certain agreement on modes of conduct and on the values determining behaviour, very considerable nonconformism of religious ideas has been allowed. It is not surprising, therefore, that many Hindus look upon even Buddhism as a branch of Hinduism.

This book is divided into two parts. The first deals with the important features of Hindu religious thought and practice, while in the second a short history of the growth of Hinduism from the earliest time has been attempted. Naturally, in a book as short as this, I have not been able to

1. *Comparative Religion*. Penguin Books, fifth edition, 1956, p. 112.

give anything like a comprehensive account of Hinduism. Instead I have tried to provide a picture of what appear to me to be the main tendencies and characteristics of Hinduism, and to study the stages through which Hinduism has passed in Indian history.

CHAPTER 2

The Nature and Growth of Hinduism

HINDU society is a product of many races and many cultures. It is necessary to recognize this fact to appreciate the complexity of the Hindu society and religion. The term Hindu is derived from the River Sindhu (the Indus), for the Persians referred to India as the land beyond the Sindhu. Hinduism would thus appear to be a generic term meaning the religions of the people of India. There is, however, a greater unity in Hinduism than this derivation would suggest, indeed Hinduism was for centuries the most important factor in preserving the unity of India. How this complex religion evolved is an interesting story. We shall give a short historical sketch in this chapter and discuss the process in greater detail in Part II of this book.

The earliest known Indian civilization is the so-called Indus Valley Civilization. There are indications that by about 2500 B.C. this urban civilization was already quite advanced. It decayed in the middle of the second millennium B.C., perhaps because of the invasion of people who described themselves as *Ārya* (Aryan). Today this term Aryan is an awkward expression, particularly because of its association with Hitler and Nazism. This is unfortunate, because Aryan is one of the most commonly used expressions in Indian history. Apart from representing a particular group of people, the term also means 'noble' or 'good'. So, just as the term has unfortunate associations in the Western mind, it has rather attractive associations in Indian thought. Some doubts have been raised as to whether there was ever such a thing as the Aryan race, but this does not really concern us. There is no doubt that in the second millennium B.C. some invaders arrived in India who called themselves Aryans, who spoke a language from which Sanskrit (as we know it) is derived, and whose religion was that presented in the

Ṛigveda. We shall use the expression Aryan to represent this group of people.

Now the religion of the Aryans, as it appears from the *Vedas*, was, on the whole, polytheistic, and the Vedic mythology seems to reveal some similarity with its European counterpart.[1] Their method of worship seems to have been the performance of sacrifices in the open air, around a fire. Nature was clearly their main preoccupation, as most of the Vedic gods were forces of nature, like the sun, the moon, fire, storm, and so on. Our knowledge of the religion of the Indus Valley Civilization is not complete, but these people seem to have worshipped deities, both male and female, that have some connexion with later Hindu mythology. One of the important indications of the gradual unification of India is the way the Aryan and the non-Aryan mythologies merge and a common mythology develops. From the point of view of Hindu philosophy, however, what is much more important is the way their different outlooks upon life influence each other, and compromises emerge – such as the philosophies of the *Upanishads*, the *Gītā*, the *Dhammapadam*, and so on.

The Aryans were a very active people, and ideas like asceticism and renunciation would have horrified them. These ideas were, however, native to the earlier Indian civilizations, as far as one can guess. The non-Vedic people did not meet around the sacrificial fire like the Aryans. Their meeting grounds, where their religious traditions were carried on, were places of holy bathing. By the beginning of the first millennium B.C. the two religious traditions seem to get together and the Vedic religion accepts ideas of renunciation, asceticism, and so on.

1. A comparison of the *Vedas* with the Iranian *Avesta*, the Greek and Roman literatures, and even Teutonic and Nordic tales (for instance the Eddic poems) reveals striking similarity between their respective mythological beliefs. For example, the Vedic god of the sky Dyaus (or Dyaus-pitar) is none other than the Greek Zeus, the Latin Jupiter, the old Norse Tyr, and the old Teutonic Ziu. The Hindu god Mitra is the same as the Iranian Mithra, whose cult became so widely diffused in the Roman empire during the third and fourth centuries A.D. Apart from mythology, their views on life and death, the earth and the heaven, seem to have much in common.

The *Upanishads* (*c.* 800 B.C.) centre around the doctrine of the *Brahman* and the *Ātman*. By *Brahman* is meant the all-pervading God. This term, for the English reader, is rather confusing, as he is likely to confuse it with *Brāhmaṇa*, a member of the priestly caste, commonly written in English as Brahmin. The term Brahmin, though phonetically wrong, will be used in this book, as it has become an English word and is perhaps easier to distinguish from *Brahman*. The other term, *Ātman*, means Self. The *Upanishads* point out that the *Brahman* and the *Ātman* are the same. The Supreme has manifested Himself in every soul, and the student of religion is dramatically told in the *Upanishads*, 'Thou art That' (*Tat tvam asi*). This idea provides the core of most Hindu religious thought and is developed later by Śaṃkara into his doctrine of *advaita* (lit., non-duality). This is a monistic doctrine, which denies the existence of the world as separate from God. In the *Bhagavad-Gītā*, however, we find a slightly different development of the Upanishadic teaching. It was composed a few centuries after the *Upanishads* (i.e. about the middle of the first millennium B.C.) and it discusses, not the unreality of the world, but man's duties in the world. The indestructibility of the soul is claimed, selfless work is put forward as an ideal, and the duties of every human being are emphasized. It is in this period (between 800 and 500 B.C.) that the main foundations of modern Hinduism are laid, polytheism gives way to monotheism, a moral code of conduct clearly emerges, and the future trends of the religion are largely determined. Meanwhile Jainism and Buddhism emerge. Both develop the Hindu ideals of renunciation and love and use the Hindu metaphysics of reincarnation, but the emphasis is considerably changed. India becomes largely Buddhist for some time, particularly from the third century B.C. under the great Emperor Aśoka. Later, Hinduism gains predominance again. Buddhism, however, leaves behind considerable influences on Hinduism – adding to its mythology, expanding its cultural content, and affecting its moral code.

Post-Buddhist Hinduism shows various trends. Hindu documents emphasize three main ways of reaching God:

jñāna (knowledge), *karma* (action), and *bhakti* (devotion). Some schools of thought, the *Advaita* Vedantists for example, emphasize the path of knowledge, while many of the movements take the path of exuberant devotion rather than that of calm appreciation of the nature of God. This is, however, by no means only a post-Buddhist phenomenon. The tradition of *bhakti* is found from the time of the *Vedas*, though it is on the whole a non-Aryan tradition. In the latter part of the first millennium B.C. the idea of the *avatāra* (Divine incarnation) develops, and this helps *bhakti*, for it is much easier for men to love a personal God than the all-pervading, abstract *Brahman* of the *Upanishads*. The *Bhakti* movement has often centred around the *avatārs*, Kṛishṇa or Rāma, though sometimes it has also been based on devotion to non-incarnate God. Even in the latter case, however, some form is attributed to the Formless and He is worshipped in the form of, say, Vishṇu or Śiva or Kālī. We shall discuss in a later chapter this Hindu tradition of giving a shape to the One beyond all shapes. The *Bhakti* movement was particularly flourishing in the Middle Ages and was reinforced by the Muslim *Sūfi* tradition.

In the modern period, partly as a reaction to Christian missionary activities, popular interest in old Hindu documents like the *Upanishads* has increased. Most Hindus of the educated classes seem to believe in the Upanishadic doctrine of the world being a manifestation of the *Brahman.* Interest in the less abstract forms of religious worship has declined among these classes and sometimes these are performed more as social customs than as purely religious activities. However, a vast majority of the economically poor Hindus approach God through traditional simple methods using the ways of devotion (*bhakti*) and of performances (*karma*) rather than the path of pure knowledge (*jñāna*). It is the continuation of these methods that is responsible for the mistaken belief not uncommon in the West that Hinduism is a polytheistic religion. If the doctrine of the *Brahman* is not understood, this is an easy mistake to make, for, in popular Hinduism, God is worshipped in different forms. Depending on the social traditions of particular sections of the people, Hindus show a particular attachment to a particular figure in Hindu mythology and worship God in that form. The Nameless and the Formless is called by different names, and different forms are attributed to Him, but it is not forgotten that He is One.[1] This idea has not been expressed only in the scriptures and the learned texts; most unsophisticated worshippers will accept its truth. This partly illustrates the unity in diversity of Indian *sādhanā*. This is what Rajjab meant, when, four hundred years ago, he sang: 'The worship of different sects, which are like so many small streams, move together to meet God, who is like the Ocean.'

1. This question is discussed further in Chapter 5.

CHAPTER 3

Social Ideals and Values

ACCORDING to Hindu doctrines, the ideal life consists of four *āśramas* (stages): *brahmacarya*, the period of discipline and education, *gārhasthya*, the life of the householder and active worker, *vānaprasthya*, retreat for the loosening of bonds, and finally *sannyāsa*, the life of a hermit. *Brahmacarya* is an active period of education and hard work. In Hindu values, *jñāna* (knowledge) and *yoga* (forms of physical and mental discipline) have always been held in great regard, and it is only to be expected that disciplined education should be considered the prime religious duty of youth.[1] *Gārhasthya* is not looked upon as a less important period of life than the later ones, even though renunciation is such an important Hindu value. In a sense *gārhasthya* is considered to be the mainstay of the four *āśramas*, for it gives unity and cohesion to the entire social structure, and the other *āśramas* depend on it for their sustenance. The Hindu is supposed to

1. It must not be assumed that according to this view of life education should consist of only metaphysics and religious instructions. A number of early Indian contributions to grammar, logic, phonetics, arithmetic, trigonometry, algebra, not to mention literature, came from religious people. The same is true of medical treatises (for example, Caraka on medicine and Suśruta on surgery) in the early centuries of the Christian era. While Hindu philosophers have tried to go *beyond* the material world, the realities of the material world were not neglected. In fact a sound knowledge of the physical world was always considered to be a part of Hindu education. 'It is necessary, therefore, that advancing Knowledge should base herself on a clear, pure, and disciplined intellect. It is necessary, too, that she should correct her errors sometimes by a return to the restraint of sensible fact, the concrete realities of the physical world. The touch of Earth is always reinvigorating to the son of Earth, even when he seeks a supraphysical knowledge. It may even be said that the supraphysical can only be really mastered in its fullness – to its height we can always reach – when we keep our feet firmly on the physical. "Earth is His footing," says the *Upanishad* whenever it images the Self that manifests in the Universe' (Shri Aurobindo. *The Life Divine*. New York, 1949, pp. 12–13).

lead an active, married life at this stage, when ideals of social living are held to apply with particular force. It is often said that the Hindu ideal is inactivity, but in fact a considerable part of the Hindu scriptures discusses the value of an active life. 'Do you perform prescribed action, for action is better than inaction, and the support of your body, too, cannot be accomplished with inaction' (*Bhagavad-Gītā*, Third Lesson, verse 8). Kṛishṇa points out to Arjuna that one must be active and discharge one's duty – but the work must be selfless, that is, not for reward or even for the supreme goal of Paradise.

However, success in the worldly second period of life is not considered sufficient. In the telling words of Bhartṛihari, 'What if you have secured the fountain-head of all desires; what if you have put your foot on the neck of your enemy, or by your good fortune gathered friends around you? What, even, if you have succeeded in keeping mortal bodies alive for ages – *tatah kim*, what then?' The successes of the material world, great as they are, are not considered sufficient, and it is here that the ideal of *moksha* or *mukti* comes in. This ideal of liberation is not a negative state. It is a state of completeness, of fullness of being, free from the bondage of *karma* and, thus, from rebirth. In Hindu metaphysics reincarnation is accepted, and *moksha* or *mukti*, like the Buddhist idea of *nirvāṇa*, is freedom from it. The Hindu is supposed to loosen his association with the social life at the third stage, *vānaprasthya*, and later to lead the life of a hermit, *sannyāsa*. In the words of Rabindranath Tagore, 'When our sense organs weaken, we urge them to keep up their efforts. Even when our grip has relaxed we are reluctant to give up possession. We are not trained to recognize the inevitable as natural, and so cannot give up gracefully that which has to go, but needs must wait till it is snatched from us.'[1] In contrast to this normal behaviour, the ideal man is supposed to retreat from mortal life gradually and think not of worldly success but of *mukti*. Renunciation, thus, becomes an important part of ideal human life.

The Hindu system of values is, as should be clear from

1. *Religion of Man*. London, 1931 p. 198.

this discussion, a complex one. It includes knowledge, it embraces active work, it emphasizes sacrifice and service to others, and it culminates in renunciation. It is this complexity that sometimes leads even well-informed foreign observers to miss some aspects of Hindu ethics. It has been suggested, for example, that in India:

> . . . the world-renouncing ascetic is the type universally admired, and his renunciation is in no sense altruistic or philanthropic, but is purely self-regarding, since it is every man's business and licence to look after his eternal welfare; and to be concerned with delivering oneself from the generally accepted chain of rebirth, and from the cycle of biological existence, is not considered to be a blemish upon one's character. Gandhiji was nobly inconsistent when he made unselfish service of his fellow-men part of the discipline to which he subjected himself in order to free his soul from the bonds of the flesh, since self-forgetful service of others is a Christian, not a Hindu idea.[1]

There is indeed some justice in this criticism of Hindu values, since renunciation for personal freedom has been one of its most widely practised aspects. There is no doubt, however, that in the complex Hindu system of values, self-forgetful service of others has been no less basic a tenet than renunciation. This has been emphasized in many Hindu texts, but particularly in that great work on Hindu morality, the *Bhagavad-Gītā*. Mahatma Gandhi mentioned that he found his ideal of service in this document. 'The man', said Kṛishṇa in the *Gītā*, 'who casts off all desires and walks without desire, with no thought of a *Mine* and of an *I*, comes unto peace. This is the state of abiding in *Brahma*, O son of Pṛithā' (Second Lesson, verses 71–2). 'In works be thine office,' said Kṛishṇa in another connexion, 'in their fruits must it never be. Be not moved by the fruits of works; but let not attachment to worklessness dwell in thee. Abiding under the Rule and casting off attachment, O Wealth-winner, so do thy works, indifferent alike whether thou gain or gain not. Indifference is called the Rule' (Second Lesson, verses 47–8). The *Bhagavad-Gītā*, ever since its composition in the first millennium B.C., has been the basic Hindu

1. Bouquet, A. C., op. cit., p. 147.

religious code of conduct, and countless generations have, like Mahatma Gandhi, been influenced by its moral values. The Buddhist and Jainist ideals of selfless work were derived from this ideal of their parent religion – though, without doubt, some Buddhist rulers, for instance Aśoka, practised it with greater vigour than most Hindu kings. There were, however, some Hindu rulers, some of the *Guptas* for example, who had a great reputation for public service. There were also some remarkably progressive acts of social service performed by Hindu religious leaders – for example, the establishment of a maternity hospital as early as A.D. 1183 by the *Śaiva* religious leader Viśveśvara. Indeed the veterinary hospital in Cooch Behar, which the English traveller Ralph Fitch[1] came across in the sixteenth century, shows that service to others did not mean service only to other human beings, but to all living creatures.

The Hindu ethic, let us repeat, is one of considerable complexity. Depending on the temperament of the person concerned and the stage of his career, his duties may differ. There are of course some universal values, like truthfulness, kindness, and love, which are considered to be everybody's duty, but man's more specific pursuits are supposed to be relative to his age and temperament. So renunciation and what is sometimes called 'other-worldliness' are not the only Hindu values. Active material service is as much part of Hindu life as contemplation and spirituality. Even the approach to the Supreme may be either through *jñāna* (knowledge), or through *karma* (work), or with the help of *bhakti* (devotion). Those who do not find prayers necessary for the completeness of their lives are free to approach Him through good deeds. For others, prayers may be a vital part of their approach to God and the path of devotion may be the best

1. 'I went from Bengala into the country of Couche. Here they be all gentiles and they will kill nothing. They have hospitals for sheepe, goates, dogs, cats, birds, and for all other living creatures. When they be old and lame, they keep them until they die. If a man catch or buy any quicke thing in other places and bring it thither, they wil give him money for it or other victuals, and keepe it in their hospitals or let it go' (*Early Travels in India*. Ed. William Foster. Oxford University Press, 1921, pp. 24–5).

path for them. For a proper appreciation of the Hindu system of values, it is essential to understand this basic assumption of 'many ways to God'.

Of course, it cannot be claimed that all the high ideals of Hinduism have always been realized. The difference between the ideals preached by the scriptures and the actual practice is not a thing unknown in other religions also. Hindus, too, have often led lives that entirely contradict their code of ethics. Fortunately, however, Hinduism (like other religions) has also throughout its history produced great reforming movements to counteract these debasing tendencies. We shall study some of these movements in the second part of this book, but it may be mentioned here that it is the Spirit of these movements that has kept the social ideals alive through the three to four thousand years of the life of Hinduism. And it is in this light that we must look at the protests against the debased ideals of their own times made by the great Hindu religious thinkers (Buddha not excluded) at various moments in history. And it is in this light again that we have to examine the challenge of the modern religious leaders like Mahatma Gandhi, Vivekananda, Tilak, and, for that matter, Rabindranath Tagore, who protested:

> Leave this chanting and singing and telling of beads! Whom dost thou worship in this lonely dark corner of a temple with all doors shut? Open thine eyes and see thy God is not before thee! He is there where the tiller is tilling the hard ground and where the path-maker is breaking stones (*Gitānjali*, poem 11).

CHAPTER 4

The Caste System

THE Hindu caste system has aroused more passion, for and against, than most other aspects of Hinduism. On the one hand there are those who are indignant at the inequality it represents, but fail to look at the system historically and refuse to see the part this stratification has played in the history of the Indian society. On the other, there are the Hindu orthodox, who refuse to see that caste divisions are matters of social significance with no essential significance to religion, and must disappear as time and age demand. They forget that some ancient scriptures do not accept caste divisions, while many others do not treat them as anything very fundamental. Indeed caste divisions, as they exist today, are very much against the basic Hindu doctrine of the all-pervading *Brahman* identified with the *Ātman*.

The caste system seems to have developed out of the multi-racial nature of Indian society. Within the boundaries of the country almost all the racial features of the world can be seen, and the majority of the people seems to be racially very mixed indeed. Before the Sanskrit-speaking Aryans arrived, India already contained various racial elements, of which the Dravidians were perhaps the most prominent. The Aryans who conquered most of India do not seem to have had much respect, at least initially, for the dark-skinned natives. This was not so much because they felt culturally superior, since the urban Indus Valley Civilization, with its script, arts, sculpture, town-planning knowledge, and other crafts, represented a more developed, though less vigorous, culture than that of the illiterate, sharp-shooting, nomadic Aryans. As conquerors, however, they must have felt more powerful, and as strong believers in the Vedic religion, with its elaborate pantheon, they may have thought themselves more right-minded. Whatever the truth, the resultant plural society with different communities, different religious beliefs, different attitudes to life, and different occupations (the conquerors formed most of the new upper classes), produced a rigid caste-structure. In all probability some sort of caste divisions already existed when the Aryans arrived, and the Aryans made the most of it.[1]

In theory there are supposed to be four castes only: *Brāhmaṇa* (Brahmin), priests and religious teachers; *Kshatriya*, kings, warriors, and aristocrats; *Vaiśya*, traders, merchants, and people engaged in other professions; and *Śūdra*, cultivators, servants, and so on. The thesis that the caste system had a racial origin is supported by the association that seems to have existed between castes and colour. There is a curious (and perhaps significant) verse in the *Mahābhārata*, the Indian epic of the middle of the first millennium B.C. Bhṛigu, in explaining the nature of castes to Bharadvāja, says: 'Brahmins are fair, *Kshatriyas* are reddish, *Vaiśyas* are yellowish, and the *Śūdras* are black' (*Mahābhārata*, *Śānti Parva*, 188, 5). However, even in those early days the races do not seem to have been by any means pure, and Bharadvāja replied: 'If different colours indicate different castes, then all castes are mixed castes' (188, 6). Interestingly enough Bharadvāja felt uncomfortable about the division and went on to ask: 'We all seem to be affected by desire, anger, fear, sorrow, worry, hunger, and labour; how do we have caste differences then?' (188, 7).

The division of the society into four castes has in all probability always been theoretical, for, from the earliest times, we find references to a much more complicated caste structure. This is also what one would expect anthropologically in a society as multi-racial as ancient India. Besides the racial element, the caste structure also had an economic element in that it represented a system of division of labour and of class-stratification. The distinction between

1. It is not clear when the idea of untouchability originated. While its scriptural backing is slender, it does not seem to be of recent origin. Quite conceivably, some form of untouchability might have existed in pre-Aryan India. It is perhaps of some significance to note that untouchability is strongest in South India and that it applies not merely to low castes *vis-à-vis* higher ones, but sometimes even between different low castes.

castes by colour is in fact rare even in the earliest literature and, as Bharadvāja pointed out, mixed complexions seem to have been represented in every caste. However, the occupational divisions with which castes were associated give us a better view of the role of castes in the working of society. It must also be admitted here that hereditary caste structure has supported the artisan skill shown by some branches of Indian labour, for skill could be passed on (and improved) from father to son; the stability of the system and the security it offered provided a firm base for operational efficiency.

According to strict theory inter-caste marriage was frowned upon, though *anuloma* marriage (where the bridegroom is of a higher caste than the bride) seems to have been acceptable. In *anuloma* marriages the children belonged to the caste of their father though there are references to cases where they belonged to the mother's caste. There is no doubt, however, that inter-caste marriages were much more common than the orthodox religious leaders would have liked. Even in the religious literature we find some mention of *pratiloma* marriage (where the bride is of a higher caste). For example, in the *Mahābhārata* (*Ādi Parva*), there is the story of King Yayāti and Devayāni of the Brahmin caste. She wanted to marry him, while he resisted the idea with the argument, 'I am a *Kshatriya*, you are a Brahmin. I am not fit to marry you' (81, 18). This did not convince Devayāni, who put forward arguments to prove that this was quite proper. Yayāti continued to argue, but did not succeed in establishing his point and ultimately had to accept the idea of marrying her. Even Devayāni's father, the Brahmin *guru* Śukrācārya, gave his consent (81, 31). There are also other examples of *pratiloma* marriage in Hindu literature.

It is significant to note that many of the best-known and most-admired characters in Hindu literature were half-castes. The famous wise man of the *Mahābhārata*, Vidura, was the son of a *Śūdra* woman. That same Vidura is described as the very incarnation of *Dharma* (*Ādi Parva*, 63, 95); it is claimed that *Dharma* became Vidura (*Āśrama Parva*, 28, 21); when King Dhṛitarāshṭra wanted religious instruction he asked Vidura to give it (*Udyoga Parva*, 33–41). The great *ṛishi* Vaśishṭha was born of a prostitute, Vyāsa of a fisher-woman, and Parāśara of a *caṇḍāla* woman.

The idea of a hereditarv caste structure is not accepted in many Hindu documents, which suggest that caste should be determined by conduct not by birth.[1] Yudhisṭhira, for example, defined Brahmins in terms of their behaviour (truthful, forgiving, kind, and so on) and pointed out that a person should not be considered a Brahmin just because he was born in a Brahmin family, nor need he be a *Śūdra* even

1. That, at least in theory, caste was looked upon as a matter of character rather than of birth alone, is clearly seen in an interesting story of *Chāndogya Upanishad* (4, 4): 'Satyakāmá, the son of Jabālā, addressed his mother and said: "I wish to become a *Brahmacārin* (religious student), mother. Of what family am I?" She said to him: "I do not know, my child, of what family thou art. In my youth when I had to move about much as a servant (waiting on the guests in my father's house), I conceived thee. I do not know of what family thou art. I am Jabālā by name, thou art Satyakāma. Say that thou art Satyakāma Jābāla." He, going to Gautama Hāridrumata, said to him, "I wish to become a *Brahmacārin* with you, Sir. May I come to you, Sir?" He said to him: "Of what family are you, my friend?" He replied: "I do not know, Sir, of what family I am. I asked my mother, and she answered: 'In my youth when I had to move about much as a servant, I conceived thee. I do not know of what family thou art. I am Jabālā by name, thou art Satyakāma.' I am therefore Satyakāma Jābāla, Sir." He said to him: "No one but a true Brahmin would thus speak out. Go and fetch fuel, friend, I shall initiate you. You have not swerved from the truth"' (English translation by Max Müller from *Hindu Scriptures*. Everyman's Library, 1938, pp. 148–9).

That the Brahmins in ancient India as a caste could, to some extent, live up to their ideals, is confirmed by the accounts of various foreign travellers. Even as late as the thirteenth century, the Italian traveller Marco Polo observed: 'I assure you that these Brahmins are among the best traders in the world and the most reliable. They would not tell a lie for anything in the world and do not utter a word that is not true.... They eat no meat and drink no wine. They live very virtuous lives according to their usage. They have no sexual intercourse except with their own wives. They take nothing that belongs to another. They would never kill a living creature or do any act that they believe to be sinful' (*The Travels of Marco Polo*, translated by R. E. Latham. Penguin Books, 1958, pp. 250–1). It seems doubtful whether *all* Brahmins in the thirteenth century were as virtuous as Marco Polo suggests. These codes of conduct, however, reflect how Brahmins were expected to behave, and at least a good proportion must have succeeded.

though his parents were *Śūdras* (*Mahābhārata, Vana Parva*, 180). The same view is expressed in various other works of Hindu literature. So when an orthodox Hindu suggests that the caste system, as we know it, is an integral part of Hinduism, he is ignoring a substantial part of India's religious literature.

Anti-caste movements can be observed at various stages of Hindu history. The schools of thought that have emphasized the path of *jñāna* (knowledge) have, on the whole, tended to be supporters of castes, for it is a path that, by its very nature, was restricted to the upper classes. The followers of the path of *bhakti* (devotion), however, have tended to be, on the whole, quite liberal on this question. The *Ālvār* poets of South India (about sixth to eighth century), whose works Rāmānuja in the twelfth century described as the *Veda* of the *Vaishṇavas*, came from very low castes. Most leaders of the *Bhakti* school throughout the country have been opposed to caste-divisions. This point will be illustrated when we discuss these movements in later chapters. The best argument against treating caste-divisions as anything more than a particular social compromise at a particular period in history was put forward by the age-old *Bhavishya Purāṇa*: 'Since members of all the four castes are children of God, they all belong to the same caste. All human beings have the same Father, and children of the same Father cannot have different castes' (*Bhavishya Purāṇa, Brāhma Parva*, 41, 45).

CHAPTER 5

Customs and Festivals

HINDUISM is a product of many cultures. Nowhere is this seen more clearly than in the pattern of Hindu social customs and festivals. Every kind of religious act, from the sacrifices of the Vedic Aryans to the rituals of primitive animist tribes, can be observed in the body of Hindu practices. The meaning of most of these customs has changed considerably over the last two or three thousand years and many of them are now purely symbolical. Nevertheless, we must study these customs since they form an important part of the life of the Hindus.

It is difficult to provide a complete list of all Hindu religious ceremonies, for they vary from area to area and from community to community of this large country. These ceremonies can, however, be classified into a number of groups according to their frequency and purpose. Some, like *prātahkṛitya* and *sandhyā*, are daily. These meditations, prayers, and rituals constitute the religious duties that the high-caste Hindu is supposed to fulfil every day. Most of these are performed at home. Some Hindus place images of gods or abstract symbols on shrines in their home for the purpose of worship. In most *mandiras* or Hindu temples some daily performances take place apart from the special ceremonies on specific occasions. These include prayers, services, and various kinds of rituals. Some Hindus go to the *mandiras* daily, some less frequently, and some never at all. Since Hinduism accepts the existence of many ways of reaching the Supreme, no particular practice is compulsory for everybody.

Some Hindus have weekly religious observances, like fasting on a particular day of the week. Some prayers and penances are performed according to the lunar calendar, e.g. at the time of the full moon and the new moon. Other observances can best be described as occasional, depending on the wishes of the performer. The *vratas* (vows) provide good examples of this. They have little scriptural backing, are performed mainly by women, and are intended normally for the welfare of the family or the community.[1] *Sāvitrī Vrata* is for the welfare of the husband, *Shashṭhī Vrata* for the well-being of the children, *Māghamaṇḍala Vrata* for sunshine in the winter months, *Pausha Vrata* for good harvests, and so on.

The annual festivals provide great occasions for religious activity. Some of these are connected with the worship of particular gods and goddesses of the Hindu pantheon. There are, for example, the *pūjās* (worship) of Lakshmī (the goddess of wealth and beauty), Sarasvatī (the goddess of learning), Kārttikeya (the god of valour), Gaṇeśa (the god of wisdom and success), Devī (the world-mother in the forms of Kālī, Durgā, etc.), Manasā (the serpent goddess), and so

1. This provides us with an occasion for a digression on the position of women in the Hindu values. The question seems to be exceedingly complex. On the one hand, the *Ṛigveda* calls upon the wife to rule supreme (*Maṇḍala* X, Hymn 85, verses 26 and 46) and the *Mahābhārata* finds them fit for worship (*Udyoga Parva*, 38, 11), on the other the Hindu law-givers treat their rights with remarkable reserve. The property rights are, on the whole, quite unfavourable to women, but it is also claimed that if women are unhappy in a society it cannot be successful in any field (*Mahābhārata, Anuśāsana Parva*, 46). Polygamy is permitted (changed now after Indian independence) and polyandry is strongly disapproved of, but Queen Draupadī marries all the five *Pāṇḍava* brothers with the approval of all the pandits (*Mahābhārata, Adi Parva*). Women are supposed to keep themselves to domestic affairs, but Arjuna's wife Citrāṅgadā is described as a heroic fighter, and there are other examples of the same (see, for instance, the *Mahābhārata, Sabha Parva*, 14, 51). The later law-givers suggest that only men have a right to higher education, but the *Upanishads* narrate many cases of women taking a leading role in discussions on the most complicated subjects. In fact, when Gārgī Vācaknavī sets two problems to the scholar Yājñavalkya, and looking at the assembled Brahmin pandits says, 'If he will answer them (my questions), none of you, I think, will defeat him in any argument concerning Brahman' (*Bṛihadāraṇyaka Upanishad*, III, 8), she certainly does not reveal any acceptance of the idea of men's monopoly over education. In the Middle Ages the position of women becomes considerably worse; there is a general retreat into purely domestic activities and there is a noticeable decline in their social status. To what extent this is due to the influence of the Muslim rule and of the Middle Eastern customs, and to what degree it is a product of an internal evolution, is difficult to say.

on. Some of them celebrate mythical events, like the birth of the Divine incarnation Kṛishṇa, or the victory of the Divine incarnation Rāma over Rāvaṇa, the king of the *Rākshasas* (demons). Others are occasions for praying to God for the well-being of one's friends and relatives. On the *Bhrātridvitīyā*, for example, sisters put sandal-wood marks on the foreheads of their brothers and wish them freedom from death. Other festivals again are connected with the economic life of the community. The *Navānna* is the harvest festival. Craftsmen celebrate *Viśvakarmā Pūjā* (the worship of the great architect of the universe) by placing tools and instruments on the altar. Finally, there are annual festivals connected with the seasons. The most picturesque of these is the *Holi*, the spring festival, when people throw coloured powder and coloured water at each other.

Some religious ceremonies are connected with the stages of life. *Nāmakaraṇa* is the ceremony for naming a child; *annaprāśana* that for weaning it; *upanayana* is the ceremony at which a high-caste boy is introduced to the rights and duties of his caste and is given his sacred thread as a symbol of his new birth (hence the term 'twice-born'); *vivāha* is the marriage ceremony; *śrāddha* (*śraddhā* = respect) the funeral. Religious ceremonies are thus performed at every stage of life.

Certain astronomical configurations are considered to be of religious significance. Quite often on those days people gather in temples, or near shrines, or at river-pilgrimages for bathing. These pilgrimage meetings sometimes also provide occasions for economic activities like cattle-shows or the sale of agricultural implements. The best-known of these gatherings is the *Kumbha*, which takes place once every twelve years, when people from various parts of India gather at four places, of which the most famous are at Allahabad and Hardwar.

The list above may give some idea of the *types* of Hindu ceremonies. It does not, however, give any idea of their enormous number. If a Hindu had to perform all of them he would have no time left for anything else in life. Fortunately all Hindus confine themselves to only a few of them, and some Hindus, such as the *Bāuls*, perform none at all.

Practices vary according to cultural background, social position, caste, sex, age, and sect. The reasons for this variety and freedom will be discussed in the next chapter.

Before closing this chapter we must emphasize two aspects of these customs and practices, to avoid any possible misunderstanding. First, we must remember that in the Hindu philosophy there is no contradiction between belief in an all-embracing, all-pervading, omnipresent God and the *pūjā* of a variety of gods and goddesses of the Hindu pantheon. In religious ceremonies the images of gods may help to focus devotion, but in theory they represent nothing more than imaginative pictures of the infinite aspects of one all-pervading God. In this connexion a three-hundred-year-old conversation between the seventeenth-century French traveller François Bernier and some Hindu pandits of Banaras is perhaps worth quoting, since it will draw attention to the essence of these practices. Bernier was shocked by the ritualism and image-worship of popular Hinduism and asked the pandits how could they tolerate such things. The pandits said in reply:

> We have indeed in our temples a great variety of images. . . . To all these images we pay great honour; prostrating our bodies, and presenting to them, with much ceremony, flowers, rice, scented oil, saffron, and other similar articles. Yet we do not believe that these statues are themselves Brahmā or Vishṇu; but merely their images and representations. We show them deference only for the sake of the deity whom they represent, and when we pray it is not to the statue, but to that deity. Images are admitted in our temples, because we conceive that prayers are offered up with more devotion when there is something before the eyes that fixes the mind; but in fact we acknowledge that God alone is absolute, that He only is the omnipotent Lord.[1]

This explanation did not convince Bernier, but it is in fact quite in line with Hindu philosophy.

Secondly, we should emphasize that the significance of these ceremonies can be appreciated only with some imagination, for without the Hindu philosophical background

1. Milford, Humphrey. *Travels in the Mogul Empire* – A.D. *1656–68*. Oxford University Press, 1914, p. 342.

the rituals are not very meaningful. This perhaps explains why many people from abroad find, even after spending many years in India, that they have very little idea of what these ceremonies are all about. It would, for example, be quite naïve to assume that a Hindu taking part in the *Sarasvatī Pūjā* (the worship of the goddess of learning) *believes* that in heaven there is a fair young lady sitting on a white swan, *viṇā* (a musical instrument) in hand (as she is frequently represented in the images made for her worship), who looks after knowledge and the arts. It would require more imagination than this to appreciate the personification of abstract concepts so popular in Hindu culture, just as it would require imagination to appreciate, say, the poetry of the *Meghadūta* (the Cloud Messenger), by the fourth-century Sanskrit poet Kālidāsa, in which a lover living in exile asks a cloud to carry his message of desperate longing to his beloved, and tells the cloud which route to take and what it will see on the way. A great part of Hindu religious practice consists of an appeal to the imagination, and in the *Īśa Upanishad* (verse 8) even God is described as a *kavi*, i.e. a seer, a term that later came to mean a poet.

CHAPTER 6

Unity and Freedom

HINDUISM accepts not only the omniscience and omnipotence of God, but also His omnipresence. He is *ekamevādvitīyam*, One without a second, and He, in the words of the *Bhagavad-Gītā*, 'dwells in the heart of all beings' (Lesson 18, verse 61). The number of paths to the One Infinite is necessarily infinite. It is this recognition of 'many paths', each valid in itself but none alone complete, that gives to Hinduism its immense variety. The religious beliefs of different schools of Hindu thought vary and their religious practices also differ; there is in it monism, dualism, monotheism, polytheism, pantheism, and indeed Hinduism is a great storehouse of all kinds of religious experiments.[1]

The *Vedas* do not accept an antinomy between *purusha* (soul, spirit) and *prakṛiti* (substance), but it is this that provides the essence of the *Sāṃkhya* philosophy. The *Sāṃkhya* rejects the idea of a personal God, but the *Bhakti* movements base their religion on devotion to God regarded mainly as a person. In contrast to both these, *Śaṃkara* and the *Advaita* school reject the idea that anything other than God exists. The Universe is His manifestation; He alone is real; the world is *māyā*. The *Rāmāyaṇa* and the *Mahābhārata* (including the *Bhagavad-Gītā*) accept the idea that God may have human incarnations, *avatāras* (such as Rāma, Kṛishṇa, or

1. 'Indian religion has always been hospitable, absorbent, and syncretistic. Hence within Hinduism as it exists there is an almost unbelievable tolerance of varieties of both belief and practice. Inside the social structure of Hinduism can be found philosophic mystics, who have no belief in a personal deity; pluralists, ranging from crude animists mainly interested in local godlings (such as the village-mother or the jungle spirit) to polytheists of the type familiar to students of Greek, Roman, and Egyptian antiquities; and, between these two extremes, fervent monotheists, who address their devotion to a single personal God, conceived in terms superficially akin to those used by many Christians' (A. C. Bouquet, in 'Hinduism', *Chambers's Encyclopaedia*. 1950, p. 98).

Buddha). This idea is not present in the *Upanishads*, and the *Vedas* would have rejected it; but, on the other hand, the *Bāuls* sing, 'As we look on every creature, we find each to be his *avatāra*.' Most schools of Hindu thought accept the Upanishadic idea of an all-pervading *Brahman*, the Supreme, but details of religious belief differ very widely indeed. So it is not doctrinal agreement that provides the unity of Hinduism.

We have mentioned earlier that *dharma* and religion are not the same, and that Hinduism is in fact a *dharma* rather than a religion in the restricted sense of the word. 'The word "civilization"', wrote Sister Nivedita (Margaret Noble), 'is a Western equivalent for our word *Dharma* or "national righteousness".'[1] 'This patience, this steadfastness, this sincerity, is *Dharma* – the substance, the selfness of things and of men' (p. 51). *Dharma* has, thus, more to do with the nature and behaviour of men than with their beliefs. It does not necessarily imply any doctrinal agreement except in so far as this influences conduct. 'While it gives absolute liberty in the world of thought,' to quote Professor Radhakrishnan, 'it enjoins a strict code of practice. The theist and the atheist, the sceptic and the agnostic may all be Hindus if they accept the Hindu system of culture and life . . . what counts is conduct, not belief.'[2] Of course, it is an open question whether attempts to unite with God should not be considered part of Hindu conduct, and it is thus perhaps debatable whether an atheist can be considered a Hindu if he otherwise follows a Hindu way of life. There can be no doubt, however, that Hinduism is basically more a matter of conduct than of belief.

Social observances can be either *lokācāras* or *śāstrācāras*. The former refers to the socially accepted rules of behaviour (*loka* = people; *ācāra* = conduct) without, necessarily, any sanction in the *śāstras* (scriptures), while the latter refers to the śāstric codes of behaviour.

Some of the *śāstrācāras* and *lokācāras* are concerned not merely with general codes of conduct (like honesty, un-

1. *Religion and Dharma*. (London, 1915), p. 51.
2. *The Hindu View of Life*. (London 1927), 1931, pp. 77 and 38.

selfish work, kindness, love, and so on), but also with details of forms of behaviour, sometimes even specifying performances and rituals. But both *lokācāras and śāstrācāras* are considered to be, ultimately, *bāhya* (external), and anyone who feels that his temperament is in conflict with the detailed performances need not feel bound by them. Thus *Bāuls* and members of certain *Bhakti* schools have often declared their rejection of these performances without denying the basic Hindu ideals. Sometimes *gurus*, or religious teachers, have recommended to their disciples the non-performance of some conventional rites, but this has not made them any less Hindu provided that Hindu ideals and the principles of the social code of conduct have not been denied. In fact the uniting factor among the enormous variety of religious beliefs and ceremonies which one finds in Hinduism has been a belief in a basic code of behaviour, including selfless work, detachment, honesty, love – that is, in the words of Kṛishṇa, 'Hateless towards all born beings, friendly, and pitiful, void of thought of a *Mine* and *I*, bearing indifferently pain and pleasure, patient' (*Bhagavad-Gītā*, Lesson 12, verse 13). To this may be added a desire to come closer to God in whatever way is found most fit.

As far as religious worship is concerned Hinduism is very free. One may try to reach God through work (*karma*), or meditation and knowledge (*jñāna*), or simply through devotion (*bhakti*). All are equally valid. The details of religious performances may vary from person to person, as may the details of religious assumptions. Since Hinduism denies the existence of any exclusive way of reaching God, this is only natural. As the age-old *Mahimna-Stotra* puts it: 'All these paths, O Lord, *Veda*, *Sāṃkhya*, *Yoga*, *Pāśupata*, *Vaishṇava*, lead but to Thee, like the winding river that at last merges into the sea.'[1] This, in fact, is the message of Hinduism, if it has one. He is infinite, omniscient, omnipotent, omnipresent, but He may appear different to different people. There are various ways of reaching Him,

1. In *Bhagavad-Gītā*, the Lord, in the form of Krishna, declares: 'However men approach me, even so do I welcome them, for the path men take from every side is mine' (Fourth Lesson, verse 11).

each as valid as every other. Apparently conflicting views of God may be nothing more than the infinite aspects of the same Supreme. Hinduism also points out that a difference of metaphysical doctrine need not prevent the development of an accepted basic code of conduct. The important thing about a man is his *dharma*, not necessarily his religion.

Part Two

HISTORICAL EVOLUTION OF HINDUISM

CHAPTER 7

The Indus Valley Civilization

RELIGION is not a product of recent times. Its origin seems to recede with the advance of historical research. It is difficult, if not impossible, to mark out the origin and development of Hinduism in India. The *Vedas* and the Vedic religion are popularly considered to be the bedrock of Hinduism and Hindu civilization, but these books contain references to earlier and different cultures and systems of values. For a long time it was in the *Vedas* themselves that one had to search for these non- or anti-Vedic references, but recently an interesting archaeological discovery has provided us with a mass of information about pre-Vedic cultures.

In 1917 an Indian archaeologist came across an ancient knife in a place called Mahenjodaro (Mound of the Dead) in the Larkana Valley in Sind. Diggings carried out in 1922 brought to light some stone seals, identical with those found at another site, Harappa.[1] Further excavations revealed clear evidence of planned communal living in cities dating from at least 2500 B.C. A number of other sites were also located which shared this pre-Vedic culture, referred to as the Indus Valley Civilization.

The men of the Indus Valley knew the use of metals and minerals such as gold, silver, copper, tin, lead, and bronze.

1. The ruins at Harappa were discovered in the nineteenth century by William Brunton, an English engineer engaged in laying out and building a railway between Multan and Lahore. Brunton's archaeological interest was not, however, excessive, and he used the ruins only for obtaining ballast for the track. Even today the trains run on a hundred miles of line laid on a secure foundation of third-millennium B.C. brickbats. General Cunningham, later Director-General of an Archaeological Survey of Northern India, also visited Harappa in 1856, when Brunton was gathering ballast. While Cunningham recognized that the discovery was important, its true significance was not understood until the Mohenjodaro ruins were found, and excavation work started only about seventy years after Brunton's discovery.

Iron, however, is absent, although the *Vedas* contain many references to iron. Among food-stuffs were found wheat, barley, fruits, meat, and fish. Cotton was grown, and weaving and dyeing were practised. The culture was largely urban, and many well-planned sets of streets and an impressive system of drains reflect the efficiency of some form of municipal government.

The civilization has left behind many works of art. Its script, as yet undeciphered, is ideographic. It seems to have had highly skilled industries and a strong merchant class. It is difficult to say which races belong to it, but there are indications of a mixture of a number of racial types. In all probability it was a pre-Aryan Indian civilization and was perhaps destroyed by the invading Aryans, who had better military equipment and more martial traditions. Alternatively it may have been destroyed by severe floods.

While communal temples seem to be rare, the civilization was certainly not secular. Many figures suggest *yogīs*. Some of the images which have been found have a close affinity to *Paśupati Śiva* of the Hindu religion. Some traces of tree, animal, and serpent worship seem to be noticeable. The worship of the mother-goddess (*Devī*) and of the mother image of spiritual power (*Śakti*) that we now find included within Hinduism perhaps came from this culture. There are numerous clay figures of women of the relevant type to suggest this. Perhaps the *Śaiva* and the *Śākta* systems had their origin in this period, and also the ways of *Yoga* and contemplation which now form an essential element of Hinduism. Whatever may be the precise nature of the contribution of the Indus Valley Civilization to the Hindu religion, there is no doubt that in those ancient times some fusion between Vedic and pre-Vedic cultures took place on Indian soil.[1]

1. Not much is known about the religious practices of those Indian people who were pre-Aryan but did not belong to the Indus Valley Civilization. It is clear, however, that some Hindu customs (e.g. the use of *sindūra*, vermilion, and *śaṅkha*, conch-shells, in some religious ceremonies) came from these people. We shall discuss other influences in later chapters.

CHAPTER 8

The Vedic Age

WE may now look at the Vedic age, which had, in many ways, a decisive influence on the trend of Indian culture. Of course, the requirements of modern life have changed many Indian customs and the elaborate sacrifices (*yajña*) of which the *Vedas* speak gradually became less important after the Vedic age. Indeed it is the doctrine of *ahiṃsā* (non-violence and non-hatred) of the heretic sects such as the *Jainas* and the Buddhists, which gained respect later. There are other non-Vedic notions to be found in Hinduism today, such as the worship of *Śakti*, the *Vaishṇava* approach through devotion or *bhakti*, and ideas of asceticism, renunciation, and continence, but the Hindu nevertheless persists in thinking of his religion as being according to the *Vedas* and in looking upon the *Vedas* as the embodiment of revealed literature.

By the *Vedas* we generally mean the Vedic *Saṃhitās*, which are collections of prayers and ritual formulae.[1] Their main heroes are the gods and the recurring motive of their worshippers is propitiation. The so-called 'way of works' (*karma vidhi*) is a way of pleasing the celestial governors of human destiny. In the course of time, rituals grew and multiplied whose meaning only the experts knew. Possibly the later search for the ways of knowledge (*jñāna*) and devotion (*bhakti*) began in a dissatisfaction with this elaborate ritualism of the Vedic religion. The birth of the *Upanishads*, with their emphasis on

1. In the strict sense, the *Vedas* (*Veda* = knowledge) consist of three parts – the *Saṃhitās*, the *Brāhmaṇas*, and the *Upanishads*. The *Saṃhitās*, which literally means collections, consist of a collection of hymns in praise of gods (the *Ṛigveda*), a collection of melodies connected with the hymns (the *Sāma Veda*), a collection of sacrificial formulae (the *Yajurveda*), and a collection of magical formulae (the *Atharvaveda*). The *Brāhmaṇas* consist of prose texts dealing with sacrifices and rites to be performed by priests and treatises on their significance. The *Upanishads* consist of discourses on the nature of the Supreme Reality and are documents of immense significance for the Hindu philosophy. They are discussed in Chapter 10.

knowledge and meditation, and of the *Bhakti* literature with its emphasis on love and adoration, were revolts against the formalism of the Vedic system. We shall discuss these developments in a later chapter.

The Vedic Aryans were divided into different groups, but they were held together by a common worship of their gods and by their ordering of religious observance. In their view, man's life was in the hands of the gods, to be killed or raised to a status equal with their own. The correct performance of sacrifices brought earthly increase and an assured comfort in the heavens above, the ideal of Vedic man. It is only in the *Atharvaveda* that one hears of men along with the gods and the heavens. This may be one of the reasons why the orthodox have always frowned upon the *Atharvaveda*; it contains references to many non-Vedic influences, such as the prayers of the outcastes (*Vrātyas*) who opposed sacrifices.

There are four *Vedas*: *Ṛik*, *Yaju*, *Sāma*, and *Atharva*. The oldest and the most important of these is the *Ṛigveda* (*Ṛik* + *Veda*). Of the different recensions only one has come down to us, which consists of 1,028 hymns divided into eight or ten books. The *Atharva* may be mentioned next in order of importance. It contains a large number of magical formulae and contains definite pre-Vedic influences. *Atharva* literally means the Fire Priest. Many of its verses are also found in the *Ṛigveda*. Some of the *mantras* do not seem to be heavily endowed with spiritual meaning, but from time to time one comes across utterances of very considerable sophistication which elevate the character of the entire anthology and make one feel that there is clearly more in it than meets the eye. The *nṛi*, *mahi*, *skambha*, and *ucchishṭa sūktas* may be mentioned as instances. In the *nṛisūkta* the object of adoration is not God but man (*nṛi* = man); the *mahi* (= earth) *sūkta* offers worship to the earth rather than to the heavens; *skambha* speaks of the secret splendour of creation; *ucchishṭa* is a hymn to superfluity.

The *Sāma* contains a large number of *Ṛik mantras*. These *mantras* used to be sung and there are instructions for the tunes. The *Yajurveda* deals mainly with works of sacrifice and is divided into two parts. Most of the Vedas had various divisions and subdivisions, not all of which have survived, partly because they were long transmitted by word of mouth.

On the time of the composition of the *Vedas*, opinions differ. Modern scholars do not consider them as ancient as the majority of Indians have done so far. Winternitz thought the *Vedas* belonged to a period stretching from 2500 B.C. to 700 B.C., but most scholars today would certainly put the origin at a date later than 2500 B.C. In a document of about 1380 B.C., the Mitannian king Mattiuaza is found invoking the gods Mitra, Varuṇa, and Indra of the Hindu pantheon; so the roots of the *Vedas* certainly stretch at least to the middle of the second millennium B.C.[1] It may be mentioned in passing that religiously-minded people often have little interest in fixing the date or the age of their beliefs. More than the history it is the revelation itself that interests the Hindu.

Most of the Vedic gods are taken from nature: the sun, the moon, fire, sky, storm, air, water, dawn, rain, and so on. Indra, the god of rain and thunder, seems to have enjoyed a greater importance than others. The hymns to the gods contain some wonderful pieces of poetry. They even include abstract notions such as sky and space deified into Prajāpati and Varuṇa. Varuṇa later changed into the god of good and evil, of the right law; Prajāpati became the one Lord of all creation, the force that runs the world. Even Faith was deified. The hymns to Night and to Forest show, besides the spiritual significance that may be attached to these largely esoteric writings, an extraordinary sensitivity to the beauties of the physical universe. The hymns to *Ushā* (dawn) and *Vāk* (speech) are equally marvellous as poetry.

The *Ṛishis* were fully aware of the importance of the subtle and the abstract. The *Atharva* contains hymns to Life and Time. Similar consciousness of the abstract is seen in the hymn to *Vāk* (speech) referred to earlier. One of the Vedic *mantras* that forms part of the daily worship of the Hindus is the *gāyatrī mantra* (*Ṛigveda*, 3, 62, 10). Its main theme is: 'We

1. See Stuart Piggott. *Prehistoric India*. Penguin Books, 1950, p. 250.

contemplate and adore the knowledge and power of the World-Creator who infuses the intellectual faculties in us.'

Yajña was the chief method of sacrifice. The performance centred around a sacrificial fire and offerings were thrown into it. On very rare occasions, offerings were thrown into water. The offerings consisted of materials of which the owner was fond and very often included things like butter, milk, meat, grains cooked in milk, intoxicating drinks, and other such items. Quite often goats were sacrificed and occasionally horses.

There are some differences of opinion on the purpose of the *yajñas*. First, *yajñas* can be looked upon as methods of pleasing gods by giving them parts of one's wealth. Secondly, *yajñas* can stand for token offerings made to gods to indicate obedience and allegiance. Finally, quite irrespective of the gods, the sacrifices can be looked upon as methods of practising renunciation. There can be little doubt that the *yajñas* began as methods of pleasing gods, and that their significance changed with time until integration with renunciation and other ideas of later Hindu philosophy was eventually achieved.

Gradually the idea of monotheism began to grow around Prajāpati and Varuna. The *Vedas* declare: 'He is one, (though) wise men call Him by many names' (*Rigveda*, 21, 164, 46). The *Mahābhārata* declares all *Vedas* to be one and the same. The Truth is one; it is our ignorance that divides it. The Supreme is not merely an architect but a creator, and He creates out of himself.[1] The universe is born of His delight. This idea of an infinite being projecting Himself in many names and forms is first mentioned in the *Samhitās* and later elaborated in the *Upanishads*. The Supreme is not bound by His creation, for His nature is freedom. The world is an expression of His play (*līlā*), His delight. We are parts of That. This identification of the *Ātman* (self) with the *Brahman* (the Supreme) is expressed in the *Upanishads* as a

1. A hymn of extraordinary sensitivity is the one called the Song of Creation. The author broods on the mysteries of creation and is awed by the enormity of the problem. See Part III (A, 2).

message to all men, '*Tat tvam asi*,' 'Thou art That.' The object of human life, according to this view, becomes unity with the Source. While this idea is developed fully in the *Upanishads*, it is in the Vedic *Saṃhitās* that one meets it first. If we look down the centuries the *Vedas* stand out as the origin of much that is noteworthy in Hinduism.

CHAPTER 9

Vedic Culture and Education

As the *Vedas* were not written down for ages, they called for remarkable memories in priests and teachers. Hence there began – in those ancient days – the custom of *pāramparya*, by which the literature was handed down orally from the *guru* (master) to the *śishya* (disciple) and so from one generation to the next. The subsidiary arts (history, legends, ballads, music, and drama), which first developed in the gatherings around the sacrificial altar, later became part of the traditional education of the cultured. These too were taught by the *gurus* in what were called *tapovanas* (forest schools). These centres of learning were set up in the seclusion of forest retreats, presumably to be far from the distractions of urban life. The students lived as members of the *guru*'s family and besides following their studies, helped in agricultural and other pursuits, so that the *tapovanas* could have economic self-sufficiency. The students probably did not pay any fees in cash, though most of them paid in kind later in their lives after achieving success. As the society was not yet very commercial, the respect with which the society looked upon the teachers was in itself a considerable reward. The regional kings very often helped these institutions, though they do not seem to have interfered much in their running. The reputation of the schools naturally varied with the reputation of the teachers, and there are many tales of students travelling long distances to study under a particular teacher.

As a result of the mingling of diverse races, ceremonies other than Vedic sacrifices gradually entered the life of the community and also of the *tapovanas*. One of these was the offerings made to the ancestors. From the *Purāṇas* and the *Mahābhārata* we find that this ancestor-worship is a later innovation and the priests who conducted these ceremonies were looked down upon by the more orthodox. Though most Hindu religious practices in later days include this show of respect to ancestors as a part of the ceremony, the attitude of the orthodox shows that it must originally have been outside the scope of the more sanctified code of the *śāstras*.

In spite of this intermingling, the Sanskrit-speaking people and the earlier inhabitants of India seem to have had different social customs and also different educational systems. While the Vedic Age shows little evidence of a rigid caste system among the Aryans, and all Aryans were entitled to take part in the sacrifices, the earlier inhabitants were largely excluded.

The Vedic ideal held up the life of the householder, who, through sacrifices and offerings, might reach the joys of heaven, which were his desire. The non-Vedic cultures must have contributed to Hinduism the ideas of renunciation and asceticism leading to *moksha*, *mukti*, or *nirvāṇa*, which were quite alien to the Aryan code of values. The Aryans were non-vegetarian and 'slaying cows for guests' seems to have been considered a highly praiseworthy act among Aryan squires. The Hindu belief in non-violence (*ahiṃsā*), which contributed to Buddhism and Jainism, is definitely of non-Vedic origin. With such different systems of values, the centres of education of the various communities were naturally different.

The educational centre of the Aryans was, to begin with, the sacrificial ground. History, legends, ballads, and drama would be told, sung, or enacted around the sacred arena, and lyrics and tales of love (like that of Urvaśī) would also be sung or recited. A more intellectual form of entertainment was the posing of riddles whose answers were given in the *Vedas*. The forest-schools developed from these sacrificial gatherings. For the non-Aryans the places for education and the interchange of ideas seem to have been the *tīrthas* (holy places, particularly places of sacred bathing). In these holy gatherings such non-Vedic cults or philosophies as *Nātha*, *Yoga*, and *Jaina* flourished. *Melās*, such as the *Kumbha Melā* near Allahabad, which are Hindu festivals held even today, are survivals of this tradition. Often there would be great meetings or unions (*mahā-yoga*), determined by astronomical calculations, in some holy place or other, which would also serve as a site for conferences of the religiously-minded. The cleavage between Aryan and non-Aryan life, thus, extended also to education. Only later, about the time of the *Upanishads*, do we find any great mingling of the two cultures and systems of thought. In this connexion, there is a significant story in the *Aitareya Brāhmaṇa*. A *Ṛishi* had two wives, one a Brahmin and the other a *Śūdra*. At one of the Vedic sacrifices he was imparting education to his son born of his Brahmin wife, ignoring the son of the *Śūdra* wife. The neglected child told this to his mother, who replied: 'We are *Śūdras*, *Mahi*'s children (that is 'children of the soil'; *Mahi* = Earth). We have no friends but the Earth.' She then called upon the goddess Earth who came and took away the child to the depths of the soil. There she taught him for twelve years, after which the learned boy returned and composed the *Aitareya Brāhmaṇa*, which forms a part of the sacred literature. This mythological tale is highly significant, for it represents the process of assimilation of non-Aryan culture into the body of Hindu thought. The *Aitareya Brāhmaṇa*, not surprisingly, brings in many new ideas. It gives a high place to purely aesthetic creation. God is the supreme artist and the arts of the earthly life derive their inspiration from the art of the Divine. As a means of worship art is not inferior to sacrifices. Elsewhere there are expressions of a love of progress which reveals a truly dynamic ideal.

Even in the age of the *Upanishads*, when the cultural streams in India were mingling, we find flourishing *tapovanas*. *Bṛihadāraṇyaka* and other *Upanishads* mention the names of many such schools. In fact another name for the *Upanishads* is *Āraṇyaka* (*araṇya* = forest). There is no doubt that these schools, where students (including girl students) from various parts of India came, played a very significant part in the propagation of Hindu culture and even in its evolution and coordination.

Education is integrally connected with the *dharma* of a community – hence these passing remarks on education in ancient India. Let us now return to the religious theme.

CHAPTER 10

Upanishads and the Gītā

THE Vedic religion, with its elaborate sacrifices, gradually gave way to the doctrine of the *Brahman* and the *Ātman* of the *Upanishads*. The date of the *Upanishads* is uncertain, but probably most of them were composed about 800 B.C. or after, but before Buddha, for he seems to have been strongly influenced by them. There are many *Upanishads*; it is generally agreed that the most important are: *Īśa*, *Kena*, *Kaṭha*, *Praśna*, *Muṇḍaka*, *Māṇḍūkya*, *Śvetāśvatara*, *Chāndogya*, and *Bṛihadāraṇyaka*. Each of the four *Vedas* has its own *Upanishad*. The initial verse of each *Upanishad*, shows its relation with a particular *Veda*.

The Upanishadic teaching centres round the doctrine of the *Brahman* and the *Ātman*. The meaning of *Brahman* is not easy to grasp. He is described as the one Divine Being 'hidden in all beings, all-pervading, the self within all beings, watching over all works, dwelling in all beings, the witness, the perceiver, the only one, free from qualities. He is the one ruler of many who (seem to act, but really) do not act; he makes the one seed manifold' (*Śvetāśvatara Upanishad*, VI, 11–12, *Hindu Scriptures*, pp. 219–20). *Ātman* means 'Self'. The main message of the *Upanishads* is the identity of the *Ātman* with the *Brahman*. The Supreme has manifested Itself in every soul. Through the cycle of births man approaches his final end – the realization of his self.

The identity of the *Brahman* and the *Ātman* is illustrated in the *Chāndogya Upanishad* by a conversation between Uddālaka Āruṇi and his son Śvetaketu. The latter has just returned after twelve years of study in a school; however, in his father's opinion, while he has read much (including the *Vedas*), he has not yet grasped this supreme truth. From the long series of instructions which his father then gives him, the following may be quoted:

'Fetch me from thence a fruit of the Nyagrodha tree.'

'Here is one, Sir.'
'Break it.'
'It is broken, Sir.'
'What do you see there?'
'These seeds, almost infinitesimal.'
'Break one of them.'
'It is broken, Sir.'
'What do you see there?'
'Not anything, Sir.'

The father said: 'My son, that subtile essence which you do not perceive there, of that very essence this great nyagrodha tree exists. Believe it, my son. That which is the subtile essence, in it all that exists has its self. It is the True. It is the Self, and thou, O Śvetaketu, art it.'

'Please, Sir, inform me still more,' said the son.

'Be it so, my child,' the father replied. 'Place this salt in water, and then wait on me in the morning.'

The son did as he was commanded. The father said to him: 'Bring me the salt, which you placed in the water last night.'

The son having looked for it, found it not, for, of course, it was melted.

The father said: 'Taste it from the surface of the water. How is it?' The son replied: 'It is salt.'

'Taste it from the middle. How is it?' The son replied: 'It is salt.'

'Taste it from the bottom. How is it?' The son replied: 'It is salt.'

The father said: 'Throw it away and then wait on me.'

He did so; but salt exists for ever.

Then the father said: 'Here also, in this body, forsooth, you do not perceive the True (*Sat*), my son; but there indeed it is. That which is the subtile essence, in it all that exists has its self. It is the True. It is the Self, and thou, O Śvetaketu, art it.'

(*Chāndogya Upanishad*, VI, 12–13; *Hindu Scriptures*, pp. 172–3)

This doctrine is far removed, though derived, from the religion of the *Vedas* and its sacrifices. The seeking of results by sacrifices, often by causing injury to other creatures, only strengthens the knots of human bondage. The goal, according to the Upanishadic view, is the realization of the Self. This realization of the one and unique *Brahman* pervading everything frees us from all shackles and we realize the Reality as *Saccidānanda* – Being (*sat*), Consciousness (*cit*), and Delight (*ānanda*). The fullness of this realization transcends the desire for heavenly comfort. This is developed also in the *Bhagavad-Gītā*. All our sufferings and the limitations imposed by our ego come from *Avidyā* (ignorance). Hence men must seek knowledge, with which hatred, injury, and greed are incompatible. Thus, the Upanishadic doctrine provides a basis for codes of moral conduct. The essence of the Upanishadic doctrine is put thus in the *Īśa Upanishad*. 'All this, whatsoever moves on earth, is to be hidden in the Lord (the Self). When thou hast surrendered all this, then thou mayest enjoy. Do not covet the wealth of any man! . . . And he who beholds all beings in the Self, and the Self in all beings, he never turns away from it. When to a man who understands, the Self has become all things, what sorrow, what trouble can there be to him who once beheld that unity?' (Verses 1 and 7; *Hindu Scriptures*, p. 207).

It is interesting to note, in this connexion, that in the post-Vedic philosophies (the *Upanishads*, the *Bhagavad-Gītā*, the Buddhist, and the *Jaina* scriptures) it is men who hold the centre of interest, the gods are subsidiary. In Buddhist art and literature, the gods hold the umbrella or shower flowers on the heads of great men, and sometimes blow the conch-shell. In the epics Rāma and Kṛishṇa are human, although, as incarnations of the Lord, they are also divine. The gods in the epics are their servants. On the whole, we notice that in this period sacrifices yield place to human ethics, monotheism replaces polytheism, and instead of the Vedic rituals we have a growing urge towards knowledge and devotion.[1]

1. The Vedic sacrifices were a monopoly of the Brahmins, but the *Upanishads* reveal an increasing dominance of the *Kshatriyas*. In the reports of many debates and conferences, the instructors are found to be members of the *Kshatriya* clans. In Vedic ceremonialism, women had a relatively inferior status, but in the *Upanishads* they enjoy equal eminence, though there were fewer prominent women than men. One of the most basic questions on life comes from the lips of a woman, Maitreyī, the wife of Yājñavalkya. 'Maitreyī said: "My lord, if this whole earth, full of wealth, belonged to me, tell me, should I be immortal by it?" "No," replied Yājñavalkya; "like the life of rich people will be thy life. But there is no hope of immortality by wealth." And Maitreyī said: "What should I do with that by which I do not become immortal?"' (*Bṛihadāraṇyaka Upanishad*, II, iv, 2–3; *Hindu Scriptures*, p. 62. See also the dialogue between Gārgī and Yājñavalkya, quoted in Part III, Ch. 3.)

We can see in this period the process of amalgamation between the Vedic and the non-Vedic elements of Indian culture. The result of this cultural assimilation is indeed startling, and as a document of religious philosophy, the *Upanishads* can hardly be surpassed. Schopenhauer wrote, 'In the whole world there is no study so beneficial and so elevating as that of the *Upanishads*. It has been the solace of my life – it will be the solace of my death.'[1] Perhaps this praise is too ecstatic, but there is no doubt that this product of around the eighth century B.C. is one of the most remarkable religious documents of all time.

In a somewhat different way, the *Bhagavad-Gītā*, which is perhaps better known in the West than the *Upanishads*, is also an extraordinary religious achievement. It is a development from the *Upanishads*, i.e. from the doctrine of the all-pervading *Brahman* identified with the *Ātman*. But the emphasis here is on action and on a code of human behaviour.

The *Bhagavad-Gītā*, or *Gītā* for short, means the Song of the Lord, and is a part of the great epic *Mahābhārata*. It opens dramatically at the battlefield of Kurukshetra, just before the battle begins, and the poem is in the form of a reported conversation between Arjuna, the great warrior on the side of the *Pāṇḍavas*, and his charioteer Kṛishṇa, who is the incarnation of the Supreme. Arjuna's conscience revolts at the thought of war and the large-scale murder it involves. On the opposing side he sees many friends and relatives, for the war is between two branches of the same royal family. Arjuna mentions his agitation to Kṛishṇa. 'I desire not victory, O Kṛishṇa, nor kingship, nor delights. What shall avail me kingship, O lord of the herds, or pleasures, or life? They for whose sake I desired kingship, pleasures, and delights stand here in the battle-array, offering up their lives and substance – teachers, fathers, sons, likewise grandsires, uncles, fathers-in-law, grandsons, brothers-in-law, kinsmen also. Though they smite me I would not smite, O Madhu-slayer (Kṛishṇa), even for the sake of empire over the there

1. Quoted by Will Durant. *The Story of Civilization*, Volume I. New York, 1942, p. 410.

worlds, much less for the sake of the earth' (First Lesson, verses 32–5). Kṛishṇa replies that as a warrior Arjuna must do his duty. From this problem of the morality of Arjuna's personal action, Kṛishṇa moves on to a discussion of the problems of individual duty and of social behaviour, and to general questions of human ethics. It is not possible or desirable to be inactive, but the important thing is not to be bound by one's work, by one's ego, by desire, or by the expectation of the fruit of one's work. 'Do you perform prescribed action, for action is better than inaction, and the support of your body, too, cannot be accomplished with inaction.' 'The state of mind consisting in firm understanding regarding steady contemplation does not belong to those, O son of Pṛithā! who are strongly attached to (worldly) pleasures and power, and whose minds are drawn away by that flowery talk which is full of (ordinances of) specific acts for the attainment of (those) pleasures and (that) power, and which promises birth as the fruit of acts – (that flowery talk) which those unwise ones utter, who are enamoured of Vedic words, who say there is nothing else, who are full of desires, and whose goal is heaven. . . . Your business is with action alone; not by any means with fruit. Let not the fruit of action be your motive (to action). Let not your attachment be (fixed) on inaction' (Second and Third Lessons).

Kṛishṇa also dwells on the immortality of the soul. 'Learned men grieve not for the living. Never did I not exist, nor you, nor these rulers of men; nor will any one of us ever hereafter cease to be. . . . Know that to be indestructible which pervades all this; the destruction of that inexhaustible (principle) none can bring about' (Second Lesson.)

CHAPTER II

Cultural Synthesis and its Influence on Indian Life

THE philosophical and speculative synthesis of the *Upanishads* was largely confined to the *élite*, and it is a pity that most modern books on this aspect of Indian culture deal only with the religious life of the more educated. The influence of many cultures on the life of the common folk and the synthesis achieved there is no less interesting. It will not be out of place, therefore, to say a few words on the popular cultures and religions of ancient India.

The *Vedas* are chary of the 'way of devotion' (*bhakti*), and the rise of the devotional cults in Hinduism can only be explained by the influence of non-Vedic cultures. According to the *Padmapurāṇa*, the school of devotion had its origins in the south, i.e. in the Dravidian country. The cult of devotion brought in a new class of *guru* in place of the older Vedic *ācāryas*; at the same time the centre of learning shifted from the sacrificial ground to the more democratic places of pilgrimage and bathing. Instead of altars there grew up temples with their special deities. The *Vedas* contain little reference to iconolatry or image-worship, so that this growth also is non-Vedic.

Of the many races of India, some are worshippers of a river, or a mountain, or particular trees and animals. Each of these cults has influenced Hinduism, at least to the extent of finding room within its large and capacious body. Gaṇeśa or Gaṇapati (the lord of the folk) is half human and half elephant. Sometimes, as a concession to mass sentiments, the Vedic sacrifices were preceded by these popular worships – certainly a wise measure on the part of the Aryan minority.

Śiva is another god of the non-Aryans who has been accepted in the Hindu pantheon. Relatively primitive tribes like the *Śabaras* and *Kirātas*, seem to have been his worshippers, though there are a few possible traces of his worship even in the urbanized Indus Valley Civilization. From a study of the process of assimilation, it appears that Śiva was accepted by the orthodox only after a good deal of hostility and opposition. The amalgamation of the cult of Śiva and phallic (*lingam*) worship, which can be observed later, certainly widened the *Śaiva* cult. Whatever may have been the initial simplicity of such a worship, its later philosophization led to quite an elaborate theory. The same may be said of the cult of Kālī, another folk goddess, who emerges as the mother-force of the universe. Images of a mother-goddess have also been found in the Indus Valley Civilization, and they may be connected with the origin of Kālī-worship. In some of the images Kālī looks quite frightening and in fact the famous thuggees were also worshippers of Kālī, but, interestingly enough, in some philosophies she becomes the merciful, all-suffering Supreme, beyond form and qualities, almost the equal of the concept of the *Brahman*.

Śiva was at first associated with Rudra, the Vedic storm god. Later, besides his association with fertility, we also find him as the lord of the *Yoga* (Yogeśvara) and the lord of the cosmic dance of creation and destruction (Naṭarāja). We can follow how Śiva, like Kālī, developed from one of the many folk-gods into a personified version of the Supreme to a particular group of worshippers. This power to sublimate an originally crude concept and to personify the Supreme in many forms seems a typical feature of Hindu religion.[1]

1. In the later Hindu mythology three gods, Brahmā, Vishṇu, and Śiva, form a kind of triad representing three aspects of the Supreme. Brahmā is the creator, Vishṇu the preserver, and Śiva the destroyer of the world, the last being necessary for further creation. We find all three activities around us and the three gods are supposed to represent the Supreme in these different roles. Of these three gods, the worship of Brahmā is possibly the oldest. In the *Vedas* we meet him as Prajāpati, Pitāmaha, and Hiraṇya-garbha. He is prominent in the *Brāhmaṇas*. But gradually his importance declines and now there are very few who will describe themselves as devotees of Brahmā, even though most Hindus will still accept him as one of the *trimurti* (three figures representing the Supreme). Brahmā's popularity declined before temple-building became a respectable Hindu activity and there are remarkably few temples dedicated to him. Vishṇu or Śiva cannot, however, have any grievance in this respect.

It may be pointed out in this connexion that image-worship and idolatry are not necessarily the same thing, though most Western observers seem to have treated the two as identical (see Chapter 5 and its footnotes). It is the spirit of inmost adoration of the Formless that is given shape in the images of the deities. Though these are used as aids in religious life, 'every Hindu hopes to escape someday from the necessity of using images'. It is the difficulty which the human mind has in grasping the nature of the all-pervading *Brahman* that often made specification and even personification necessary.

It is interesting to note that the *Vedas*, though accepting many gods, are without idols or images. The fact that the Indus Valley Civilization had many images shows that image-worship is a contribution of the non-Vedic cultural trend. Some attribute its rise to Greek influence on India, which was strong after Alexander's invasion. It is believed that the Greeks, under Buddhist patronage and inspiration, made the first images of the Enlightened One. This thesis does not seem to be fully satisfactory, as there was image-worship in India even before the Graeco-Buddhist *Gāndhāra* school of sculpture developed. In fact evidence of image-worship in Mahenjodaro suggests that it has existed in India at least since the third millennium B.C. There is no doubt, however, that Buddhism of the *Mahāyāna* school enriched Hindu image-worship.

A characteristic of Hindu images is that the deities, according to the canons, must always be represented as youthful. There are no old gods in India. Moreover the chief aim of the image-maker was the expression of *bhāva* or emotion rather than anatomic precision.

Along with image-worship, another characteristic of popular Hinduism is the existence of detailed codes of conduct, regulations, and observances. The *ahiṃsā* cult, particularly that of the Buddhist and the *Jainas*, turned a large section of the Hindus into vegetarians. There is also so large a number of rituals and customs of religious significance that it sometimes astonishes foreign visitors. It is interesting to note in this connexion that the thirteenth-century Italian traveller Marco Polo was surprised not only by the customs of worship in India, which appeared to him to be idolatrous, but also by the rules of the Indian religious code of behaviour. 'Another of their customs', wrote Marco Polo, 'is that all of them, male and female, wash their whole body in cold water twice a day – that is, morning and evening. . . . Likewise they drink only out of flasks, each one from his own; for no one would drink out of another's flask.'[1]

Many of the tabus were obviously inspired by sanitary and hygienic considerations. Nomads do not need the regulations that are essential for an agricultural or urban community. In the Vedic period, when the invaders first took to agricultural pursuits, we find mention of diseases that were the results of careless collective living. Later on, in the age of the *Smṛitis* (the Codes, as distinguished from the *Śruti*, the Vedic revelations), there grew up a large body of rules and regulations. These civic rules worked within the religious framework and sometimes even had religious sanction. Besides these hygienic rules, however, the peculiar traditions of various tribes and sects were also absorbed into the body of Hindu religious observances, though their historical origin often lay in crude beliefs in myths and magic.[2]

Besides absorbing popular customs, Hindu orthodoxy also gradually accepted many popular deities. The changes in the Hindu mythological universe from the days of the *Vedas* constitute a very interesting field of study. Also, instead of Vedic sacrifices (*yajña*), the common method of religious performance today in most parts of the country is *pūjā* or worship, which probably came from the Dravidians. Disciplines, such as *Kāyā Yoga* (*Kāyā* = frame or body), held that the ultimate mysteries reside in the psychic centres, or *cakras*, the opening of which became the recognized aim of strenuous practices. All these seem to reflect the influence on

1. English translation by R. E. Latham. Penguin Books, 1958, p. 239.

2. The origin of the holiness of the cow in popular Hinduism is not quite certain. The Aryans loved to eat beef, though they seem to have admired the cow as a very useful animal. The importance of the cow in India's rural life may have something to do with the question.

the body of Hinduism of popular methods of religious performance.

The Vedic chants are all in praise of the gods, who remain for ever objects of propitiation. In the epics, which we discuss in a later chapter, the universe of adoration becomes homocentric; the *Rāmāyaṇa* and the *Mahābhārata* speak of men and their greatness. The mediator between God and men is the *avatāra* or the Divine incarnation. This doctrine of the *avatāra* is non-Vedic and possibly non-Aryan,[1] and it seems to be an advance on the dependence on the extra-human gods of the Vedic period. It is a little amusing that Indra, the powerful Vedic god, appears in the *Chāndogya Upanishad* as a student of the doctrine of the *Brahman* and grasps the sophisticated doctrine only with considerable difficulty (*Chāndogya Upanishad*, VIII, vii–xv). The cultural influences of the non-Aryan certainly humanized the Vedic religion.

1. The origin of the concept of *avatāra* is obscure. It cannot be found in the *Vedas*, but it is possible that it came from the Aryan settlers in Iran. The idea of discontinuous incarnations can be found in the *Bahrām Yāsht*, which forms part of the Zoroastrian corpus, where incarnations of the deity Verethragna can be seen. According to another theory, the concept originated in central Asia, as the *Bāhram Yāsht* shows traces of Chinese influence and mythology. In none of these beliefs, however, does the concept play as important a part as it does in post-Vedic Hindu thought, particularly that of the epics, *Rāmāyaṇa* and *Mahābhārata*. Since Kṛishṇa, the incarnation of the Lord, who is supposed to reveal Himself in the *Bhagavad-Gītā*, is a non-Vedic non-Aryan Indian deity, it is not at all improbable that the concept of the *avatāra* was present in non-Aryan Indian thought for a long time.

CHAPTER 12

Jainism and Buddhism

WE have seen in the last few chapters how Vedic and non-Vedic forms of culture were being combined in India to form new cultural trends round about 800 B.C. This period of cultural evolution was thus full of heterodox creeds and opinions. There developed, among other schools of thought, the *Lokāyata*, of which Cārvāka was the best known teacher. This school considered physical sense data to be the only source of knowledge. Naturally it challenged the whole of Hindu metaphysics.[1] One of the Cārvāka aphorisms became a well-known Indian proverb: 'Live well, as long as you live. Live well even by borrowing, for, once cremated, there is no return.' This rejection of after-life and reincarnation can be found also in the teaching of some pandits in the epics. In the *Rāmāyaṇa* we meet a Brahmin called Jāvāli who advises Rāma, the hero of the epic, not to give up his kingdom.

I grieve for those who, abandoning the pleasures of the world, seek to acquire merit for felicity hereafter and sink to an untimely death, I do not grieve for others. Men waste food and other precious things by offering them up yearly, as sacrifices in honour of their departed ancestors. O Rāma, has a dead man ever partaken of food? If food that is eaten by one, nourishes another, then

1. See R. Garbe. 'Lokāyata', in *Encyclopedia of Religion and Ethics*. Ed. Hastings, Vol. VIII. 'There are clear indications of the presence in India, as early as pre-Buddhistic times, of teachers of a pure materialism; and undoubtedly these theories have had numerous adherents in India from that period onwards to the present day. . . . The Lokāyata allows only perception as a means of knowledge, and rejects inference. It recognizes as the sole reality the four elements, i.e. matter, and teaches that, when a body is formed by the combination of elements, the spirit also comes into existence, just like the intoxicating quality with the mixture of special materials. With the destruction of the body the spirit returns again into nothingness. . . . The *Vedas* are declared to be the idle prating of knaves, characterized by the three faults of untruthfulness, internal contradiction, and useless repetition' (p. 138).

those who journey need never carry provision on the way. Relatives might feed a Brahmin, in his name, at home!

O Rāmacandra, these scriptural injunctions were laid down by learned men, skilled in inducing others to give, and finding other means of obtaining wealth, thus subjugating the simple-minded. Their doctrine is 'Sacrifice, give in charity, consecrate yourselves, undergo austerities, and become ascetics'. O Rāma, be wise, there exists no world but this, that is certain! Enjoy that which is present and cast behind thee that which is unpleasant! Adopting the principle acceptable to all, do thou receive the kingdom offered thee by Bharata (*Rāmāyaṇa*, Ayodhyā Kāṇḍa, 108).[1]

The challenge of these agnostics or atheists had a beneficial effect on Hindu thought, for it forced the religious leaders to defend their views, reconsider their positions, and even perhaps get rid of some of their doubtful practices. It was in this period of heterodoxy also that Jainism and Buddhism were born. The Vedic interest in gods had by then been replaced by interest in man and in human greatness; and the Vedic ideal of a pleasant life in heaven had been challenged by believers in renunciation, ego-lessness, and selfless work. The theory of the transmigration of souls and the theory that life gradually evolves, through many births, towards its ultimate realization had been developed by the *Upanishads*. On the other hand materialists had begun to question the existence of God perhaps even as early as the Upanishadic period. In this atmosphere of intellectual experimentation Jainism and Buddhism arose, and the effects of current thought are readily seen in these religions. The founders of both were *Kshatriyas*, not Vedist Brahmins, and both creeds arose in the eastern provinces far removed from the centre of the Vedic culture.

The *Jainas* accept twenty-four teachers of *tīrthaṅkaras* previous to Mahāvīra, who consolidated the *Jaina* faith. Mahāvīra and Buddha were near contemporaries and there is a certain similarity in their teachings. Both were anti-Vedic and also rejected the caste system. Like Buddhism, Jainism also aims at escaping from the cycle of births. To

1. English translation from H. P. Shastri. *The Rāmāyaṇa of Valmiki*. Vol. I. London, 1952, p. 389.

this end three ways or 'jewels' are necessary – right faith, right knowledge, and right conduct. The *Jaina* code of conduct includes five vows: not to kill; not to speak untruth; not to steal; continence; and the renunciation of pleasure in external objects. Rajputana, Gujerat, and some parts of South India are still strongholds of the *Jaina* faith, and at one time it was prevalent in many other parts of the country, for example in Bengal in its pre-Buddhist period. Jainism contributed to Hindu thought and practices to a very considerable extent. The well-known austerity of *Jaina* ascetics had its impact on Hindu traditions. Vegetarianism of some sects of Hindus may be due to Jaina influence. Another contribution of Jainism, which is not often recognized, is its part in the growth of medieval mysticism. Though Jainism started as a simple faith free from the rule of priests and pandits, it gradually became more priest-ridden later. Even image-worship became a part of later Jainism. As a reaction to this, many movements were formed in the fourteenth and fifteenth centuries with the aim of returning to the simple faith. The names of Tāran Swāmi and Lunkā Shāh may be mentioned in this connexion. Rāmamuni's famous 'Pāhuḍa Dohā' is perhaps the first example of the simple mystic poetry of the Middle Ages. This medieval mysticism, which we shall discuss in a later chapter, was an important facet of Indian culture.

It is perhaps unnecessary to discuss Buddhism in detail in this book, especially as there is already a most readable book on Buddhism by Christmas Humphreys in this Pelican religious series. Buddha was born in the sixth century B.C., as Gautama Siddhārtha, the son of the king of the *Śakya* clan, at the foothill of the eastern Himalayas. The tragedies of human existence made him restless and he left the palace in search of truth some time after his first child was born. The great renunciation of the Buddha has remained, to countless generations in India, a most vivid symbol of the renunciation of material pleasures.

At first Gautama followed the accepted methods of spiritual knowledge by studying under noted sages and by practising ascetism and austerity. But these did not satisfy him. At last, sitting in meditation under a tree in Gayā, he saw the light. The basic tenets of Buddhism are well-known, and they included the doctrine of the Middle Path (avoidance of extremes); non-violence; non-hatred; friendliness to all; renunciation; continence; and the ideal of reaching *nirvāṇa*, the freedom from the cycle of births. The influence of the *Upanishads* on Buddhism is obvious, but Buddha gave a new turn to the development to their thought. The appeal of this dynamic creed was strong enough to convert millions in Ceylon, Burma, China, Japan, and many other countries to Buddhism. In India it became the state religion in the third century B.C., at the time of Aśoka, who spread it inside the country through various schools and through his famous rock-edicts, and also sent the first Buddhist missionaries outside the land. The story of Aśoka's acceptance of Buddhism is a typical instance of the spread of the faith. Following the footsteps of his father and grandfather, Aśoka further consolidated his Indian Empire by defeating the king of Kaliṅga, but the horrors of the battle so shocked him that he took to the non-violent and humanitarian religion of Buddhism.

Buddhism has exercised an enormous influence on the Hindu faith. In a sense it is wrong to say that Buddhism disappeared from India later. In fact most of its tenets came to be accepted by large sections of the Hindus, and Hinduism once again revealed its remarkable power of assimilation by making Buddhism a part of itself. Buddha is still accepted by the Hindus as one of the *avatāras* spreading Enlightenment to all creatures, and the fact that Buddhism had so much in common with the *Upanishads* of course made this assimilation easier.

Apart from the influence of Buddhism on Hindu religious thought, the Hindus also adopted the Buddhist method of using parables for religious instruction.[1] This can be seen in

1. The Indian mind has always been very fond of fables, and the important part which parables play in Buddhist literature is largely due to the country of its origin. Indian fables seem to have had considerable influence outside the country through other channels as well. Max Müller, Rawlinson, and others have tried to show that even some of Aesop's fables were derived from Indian fables, which is not improbable

the *Purāṇas* and also later in the stories of the *Pañcatantra*, whose literary value, quite apart from their wisdom, is very great indeed. Similarly Buddhist art also influenced the Hindus; the influence of Buddhist sculpture on Hindu iconography, for example, is readily recognizable. But perhaps the sphere in which Buddhism contributed most to Indian cultural evolution was in education. In the Upanishadic period, while there was a good deal of study and research at a somewhat decentralized level in the *tapovanas* and the princely courts, there were no organized universities. Under the influence of Buddhism various universities grew up on Indian soil, of which perhaps the most important was at Nālandā in East Bihar. Its excellence was such that it attracted students from China, Japan, Tibet, and other distant lands. Apart from religious subjects (both Buddhist and Hindu), it offered instructions in secular subjects like medicine, agriculture, dairy-farming, logic, grammar, architecture, and art. The account of the university given by Hsuan-Tsang, a seventh-century Chinese student, is fascinating. This educational development, which was the result of the Buddhist desire to spread Enlightenment, had a decisive influence on Indian cultural evolution, and naturally had a significant effect on the trend of Hindu thought. Śaṃkara, one of the most important figures of the Hindu revival after the Buddhist period, was very keen on organized educational systems. He also started religious orders or *maṭhas* for

in view of the predominance in Aesop's fables of animals like lions, tigers, elephants, peacocks, monkeys, etc., common in India, and in view of the similarity of the tales. This has not, however, been conclusively proved, nor can one see how it ever can be. There is no doubt that the European and Arab fables of the Middle Ages were strongly influenced by Indian tales. Stories of the *Pañcatantra* were translated into Persian in the sixth century and into Arabic in the eighth century as the *Fables of Pilpay.* In this Arabic translation it spread through the Islamic world and also reached Europe. A German version of these animal fables, made in 1481, was one of the earliest printed books in Europe, and Caxton's printing press provided an English version. La Fontaine in his *Fables* (1678) says in the Preface, 'It is not necessary that I should say whence I have taken the subjects of these new fables. I shall only say, from a sense of gratitude, that I owe the largest portion of them to Pilpay, the Indian sage.'

Hindu *sannyāsīs* (monks) in the style of the Buddhist *saṃghas*. The heterodoxies of Indian materialism, Jainism, and Buddhism all seem to have left their impressions on the philosophy and practices of the Hindus.

CHAPTER 13

Some Other Non-Vedic Systems

IN India there have been many sects outside the Vedic fold besides the Buddhists and the *Jainas*. In the story of the life of the Buddha himself we meet many such systems of worship. It is not possible here to discuss all these sects, but we ought perhaps to say a few words about the *Nātha*, *Yoga*, and *Siddhācāra* cults, because of their wide prevalence in India at one time.

The *Nātha* cult is closely connected with the doctrines of *Yoga*. It is also linked with the worship of Paśupati Śiva, i.e., with the worship of Śiva as the Lord of the animals. Among the Indus Valley relics, the Paśupati icon and images of *Yogis* have been found, which suggests that the cult may be very old indeed. Later all these cults came into close contact with Buddhism, Jainism, and popular Hinduism.

The Buddhists and the *Jainas*, with their ethical practicality, had installed men in the place of the Vedic gods. The *Nāthas*, *Yogis*, and *Siddhācāryas* went a step further and claimed to find all the religious mysteries in the human body itself. They spoke of what they called the solar and the lunar currents within the nervous system, the *iḍā* and the *piṅgalā*. By uniting these currents it was supposed possible to open the *cakras*, the psychic centres of the body. These *cakras* are first mentioned in the *Atharvaveda*; so some of these beliefs may be linked up with that period. Another of their concepts is the equilibrium of Śiva and Śakti, the male and the female deities representing two different aspects of the Divine force. Some elements of phallic worship can also be found among these cults. Śiva, as we have mentioned earlier, is of course particularly connected with this worship of fertility. The versatility of Śiva in different schools of Hindu thought is indeed interesting. We find him in the Indus Valley as Paśupati (Lord of the animals). We find him some time later associated with Rudra, the Vedic storm god. We discover him later connected with phallic worship. We also find him connected with the discipline of *Yoga* as Yogeśvara and as the Supreme creator and destroyer, Naṭarāja, the Lord of the cosmic dance of creation and destruction of the Universe. In many images he is depicted as the one who causes terror and makes us conscious of the destructive forces of the universe. This attitude of fear can be seen in the prayer to Rudra 'Slay us not, for thou art gracious'. At the same time in Indian literature and poetry, Śiva often appears as a loving (and beloved) god, and other examples of a quiet and domesticated Śiva can be found in folk traditions. Perhaps all this is only natural and represents the Hindu idea of infinite aspects and manifestations of the all-embracing Supreme.

To return to the cults we are discussing, the *Yogīs*, though very mystical in outlook, also produced considerable studies in physiology and medicine. Even today the *Yoga* system of exercises has great practical value and is quite commonly practised. The tradition of these cults also produced the *Tantras.*[1] The *Tāntrikas* were also believers in *Yoga* and the opening of *cakras*, and worshipped Śiva-Śakti, or, more usually, Devī, the mother-goddess. Some of the *Tāntrika* practices seem more than a little extraordinary and sometimes include elements of sexual perversion. There are, however, other aspects of the system which are more interesting from the religious point of view. The collection of *Tāntrika* lore is called *Saṃhitā* or the *Āgamas*, which means that it has come from before (through a long line of teachers and disciples). The *Āgamas* has four *aṅgas* (limbs) or portions. The first limb is knowledge. Here it is closest to the *Upanishads*. The *Brahma* doctrine that we find in the *Mahānirvāṇa Tantra* is a mixture of the philosophies of the *Upanishads* and the *Sāṃkhya*. The second limb is *Yoga*. *Kriyā*, or practices, form the third limb. The fourth is *Caryā*, or conduct or character, which deals with man's social and personal conduct. Some verses of *Mahānirvāṇa Tantra* (see in particular

1. See Arthur Avalon. *Principles of Tantra*. Part I, London, 1914, and Part II, London, 1916.

Chapter 8) throw very interesting light on these codes of conduct, sometimes reminding one of the Codes of Manu which had such a decisive influence on Hindu laws. In Chapter Fourteen of the *Mahānirvāṇa Tantra* we have some verses on the seeker free from mortal bonds that are comparable with the Vedantic notion of the *jīvanmukta*, the ideal of the living 'liberated' man.

Women play an important part in the *Tantras*, which, unlike many branches of orthodox Hinduism, do not allot women an inferior status in religious matters. They are also quite liberal in matters of social and caste restrictions. While one meets considerable intellectual sophistication in some *Tāntrika* texts, the *Tantra* has been mainly a folk religion. Other folk religious traditions such as the medieval mysticism, the *Bhakti* cult, and the *Bāul* movement will be discussed in later chapters.

CHAPTER 14

Rāmāyaṇa, Mahābhārata, and the Purāṇas

PURĀṆA literally means something that is old and was used to refer to popular, traditional texts (often legends) that had existed for a long time. In the *Vedas* there are only a few hints about many *Purāṇas* that used to be recited in religious ceremonies, and it is very difficult to make out from these scanty references what these old *Purāṇas* were like. Most *Purāṇas* were composed at later dates, though often they were based on earlier sources of which at least some were pre-Vedic.

Most famous of these are the two epics – the *Rāmāyaṇa* and the *Mahābhārata*. It is difficult to date these epics, as they were not the product of one or a few authors, but the results of the combined effort of poets of many generations. Stories were developing and verses being composed perhaps throughout the first millennium B.C., though in all probability they took their present form between the fourth century and the second century B.C. This dating is, however, by no means certain, and some scholars have suggested that the composition dates from earlier. The method of transmission, following the Vedic tradition of drama, songs, and recitation, was, for a long time, oral. They were compiled and written down perhaps a few centuries after Christ. The *Rāmāyaṇa* has about 24,000 couplets and the *Mahābhārata* about 90,000. The latter is, therefore, about seven times the length of the *Iliad* and the *Odyssey* put together. The basic story of the *Mahābhārata* is that of a conflict between two branches of the same family – the *Kurus* and the *Pāṇḍavas* – about the right of succession. The *Pāṇḍavas* are depicted with greater sympathy; but some members on the *Kuru* side command our respect, while some of the heroes on the *Pāṇḍava* side reveal remarkable human failings (for example the passionate love of gambling of the otherwise saintly character Yudhisṭhira). A striking feature of the *Mahāb-*

hārata is the unity of Indian culture it presents. The cultural traditions of different parts of this large country are described with sympathy and pride, and a gradually growing conception of a unified Indian culture is clearly revealed. The *Rāmāyaṇa* is mainly the story of the great and just king Rāma, whose wife Sītā is taken away by force by the king of Ceylon, Rāvaṇa, and is later rescued by Rāma after defeating Rāvaṇa's forces. The *Rāmāyaṇa* lacks the immensity of the *Mahābhārata*, but it too is a rich storehouse of material about Indian cultural traditions. The *Mahābhārata* may perhaps be the story of the war for the overlordship of northern India, while the *Rāmāyaṇa* looks like the story of northern influences spreading to the south.

It should be obvious from the length of the two epics that they do not tell only the basic story. Many subsidiary stories have been interpolated in the form of incidental tales told by the characters of the main narrative, sometimes for amusement and sometimes to illustrate points under discussion. Stories about *Śakuntalā*, *Nala* and *Damayantī*, *Sāvitrī* and *Satyavān*, and thousands of other fascinating narratives are found in these epics, particularly in the *Mahābhārata*. Unfortunately we cannot here go into a more detailed discussion of the nature of Indian culture revealed by these epics, but must confine ourselves to their basic religious elements.

These epics constitute one of the main sources of our knowledge of popular religious practices. Some of the beliefs and traditions of popular religion discussed in earlier chapters were from the epics. But the specifically *Rāmāyaṇa-Mahābhārata* form of Hindu philosophy is the doctrine of the *avatāra*, the Divine incarnation in human form.[1] The two Divine incarnations that appear in the epics are Rāma, the

1. Unlike Christianity which accepts only one unique Divine incarnation in Jesus Christ, Hindus accept many incarnations of God. In the *Bhagavad-Gītā* the Lord says: 'For whensoever the law fails and lawlessness uprises, then do I bring myself to bodied birth. To guard righteousness, to destroy evildoers, to establish the law, I come into birth age after age' (Fourth Lesson, verses 7 and 8). While some Hindus take the doctrine literally and accept figures like Rāma, Kṛishṇa, and Buddha as actual incarnations, others prefer to treat it as a useful myth.

hero of *Rāmāyaṇa*, and Kṛishṇa, the friend of the *Pāṇḍavas*. Unlike the superhuman gods of the Vedic *Saṃhitās* which represent natural forces (the Sun, Storm, Fire, etc.) on the one hand, and the abstract Upanishadic concept of the all-pervading formless *Brahman* manifesting Itself in various forms and shapes on the other, the *avatāras* in the epics are the human intermediaries between the Supreme and mortals. This concept had a great impact on Hindu religious life, for here God is assumed to manifest Himself in a form that can be appreciated even by the least sophisticated. Rāma and Kṛishṇa have remained for thousands of years the beloved and adored expressions of the Divine. No doubt the Upanishadic concept of the all-embracing *Brahman* (identified with the Self, *Ātman*) is, in a sense, a product of a more mature mind, but the concept of the *avatāras* has certainly had a greater influence on the average Hindu mind. Interestingly enough it is from Kṛishṇa, the *avatāra*, in the *Mahābhārata*, that we get a re-statement (and development) of the Upanishadic doctrine of the *Brahman*. This is the well-known *Bhagavad-Gītā*, which we have discussed earlier. The two elements of Hindu thought can be clearly seen in Kṛishṇa's personality; he sometimes speaks for the all-pervading *Brahman*, giving expression to the abstract Upanishadic philosophy, but at other times he speaks as a human being, as the friend of Arjuna, giving him the practical advice of the hour.

The epics also contributed to the formation of a moral code of conduct. The honesty, sincerity, and love of his fellow creatures that we find in Rāma, the chastity and kindness of Sītā, the brotherly affection of Lakshmaṇa and Bharata have been archetypes of conduct for many generations. Similarly, in the *Mahābhārata*, the self-sacrifice of Bhīshma, the truthfulness and forgiveness of Yudhisṭhira, the love of justice and the desire to protect the weak from the strong of the *Pāṇḍava* brothers, and the generosity of Karṇa on the side of the *Kurus* have provided ideals to countless Indians for many generations. The fact that all these characters reveal human weaknesses in other respects has made them more lovable and lifelike. The just king Rāma at one stage is mistakenly suspicious of his wife's chastity, the saintly prince Yudhisṭhira is fond of gambling, the heroic Arjuna has traces of vanity about his own greatness. All these make the characters human. This is also connected with the Hindu ideal of toleration and the acceptance of the notion that even the most virtuous have weaknesses.

Besides these examples of good moral conduct, the epics also contain many *discussions* of moral codes of conduct. The *Gītā* tells us of the virtues of action and knowledge and, by suggesting that human efforts should be treated as a duty, not undertaken for their 'fruits', the *Gītā* puts forward an ideal of selfless work which has influenced hundreds of generations of Indians, including, in the modern age, men like Tilak and Mahatma Gandhi. As far as details of codes of conduct are concerned, most stimulating discussions can be found in the chapters called *Śānti Parva* and the *Anuśāsana Parva* in the *Mahābhārata*. Incidentally, while the epics show a hardening of the caste system, which was not strong in the Vedic days, they also contain a remarkable number of heroes from the lower castes. Vidura, one of the wisest men at the court of the *Kurus*, is the son of a *Śūdra* maidservant. The proud Brahmin Kauśika is humbled by the religious butcher of Mithilā (*Mahābhārata, Vana Parva*, 206–14). In fact the author (or compiler) of *Mahābhārata* is himself described as the son of a fisherwoman. The epics also portray some remarkable women, like Draupadī and Gāndhārī, who provide examples not merely of chastity and devotion to their husbands but also of wisdom and justice, and sometimes even valour. Gāndhārī is the mother of the *Kuru* brothers fighting the *Pāṇḍavas*, but sympathizes with the *Pāṇḍavas* because they are in the right, and she rebukes her husband for being weak with their sons. Arjuna's wife, Citrāṅgadā, is depicted as a heroic fighter. In spite of all this, however, the *Mahābhārata* and the *Rāmāyaṇa* show the predominance of men, and the society they depict is definitely patriarchial. Polygamy seems to be quite common, particularly in the *Mahābhārata*, but curiously enough there is also one case of polyandry. Draupadī marries all the five *Pāṇḍava* brothers.

The epics provided material for literature, drama, songs, and folk-lore for thousands of years. Most Sanskrit writers of subsequent periods took stories from the *Mahābhārata* as their theme. Even for the less sophisticated, the epics were storehouses of stories and tales, and most branches of folk art were strongly influenced by them. Gradually they spread together with Indian influences outside India to Indonesia, Cambodia, Siam, and other parts of south-east Asia, where their influence can be traced in art, literature, drama, and religion. The stories of the epics sometimes show slight variations in these foreign versions, and it is an interesting study to trace the sources of alterations.

These epics do not exhaust the *Purāṇas* and there are in fact a vast number of other volumes of considerable religious significance. Of these perhaps the most important are the *Vishṇu Purāṇa* and the *Bhāgavata*. The first takes the form of a dialogue between a teacher (Parāśara) and his disciple (Maitreya). The teaching of the *Purāṇa* is summed up by Parāśara as that 'the world originated from Vishṇu; it is in Him that the world exists as a harmonious system; He is the sole sustainer and controller of the world, and in truth, the world is He' (*Vishṇu Purāṇa* I, i, 35). It is explained that God is called by different names by different people, but He of course is one, and the only one. The world is His playful manifestation (*līlā*). The One without attributes (*nirguṇa*) joyfully expresses Himself as the world full of colour, sound, touch, and other qualities (*saguṇa*).

The philosophy of the *Bhāgavata* is fundamentally the same as that of the *Vishṇu Purāṇa*. It accepts that the world is a manifestation of Vishṇu and that the same one eternal Spirit is called Brahman, Param-Ātman, and Bhagavat. The doctrine of *līlā* is used to explain the creation. The theory of *avatāras*, that is of human incarnations of God, plays an important part in the *Bhāgavata*. While it is maintained that *avatāras* are countless, Kṛishṇa received preferential treatment as the most perfect Divine incarnation. In fact most of this *Purāṇa* is about Kṛishṇa and his devotees.

The social and political ideas of the *Bhāgavata* have not received as much attention from the scholars as they ought to. Some of these ideas sound distinctly modern. It is maintained, for example, that people have a right to demand as much of the basic necessities of life as they need; to amass wealth is theft and should be punished (*Bhāgavata*, 7, 24, 8). In some fields, the *Bhāgavata* also expresses considerable rationalistic thought. To some people praying to Indra, the Vedic god of rain, for a good harvest, Kṛishṇa says, 'Being driven by vapour, clouds pour rain everywhere, on which people live. What can Indra do?' (*Bhāgavata*, 10, 24, 23). As a religious document, the *Bhāgavata* is of immense interest, since it reveals in considerable detail a very attractive philosophy of life.

CHAPTER 15

The Six Systems of Philosophy

INDIAN religious thought has expressed itself in a number of philosophies. From the point of view of Hindu theology, a study of the philosophies of the *Sūtra* period is of considerable interest. Most of these schools of thought were fully developed after about A.D. 200, though the origin of the systems can be traced to much earlier periods, sometimes as early as 800 B.C.

The main systems of philosophy of the *Sūtra* period are: *Nyāya*, *Vaiśeshika*, *Sāṃkhya*, *Yoga*, *Pūrva-Mīmāṃsa*, and *Vedānta*. Of these, the *Nyāya* and the *Vaiśeshika* form one group, the *Sāṃkhya* and the *Yoga* have much in common, and the *Pūrva-Mīmāṃsa* and the *Vedānta* are related to each other.

The *Nyāya* deals mainly with logical methods and the *Vaiśeshika* mainly with the nature of the world, but each accepts the other's conclusions. The *Vaiśeshika* uses the analytical methods of the *Nyāya* and the latter accepts the former's thesis of an atomistic constitution of the world. There are four sources of knowledge, according to the *Nyāya*: perception (*pratyaksha*), inference (*anumanā*), analogy (*upamāna*), and credible testimony (*śabda*). The principle of causation is accepted by the *Nyāya* school, but considerable attention is paid to problems arising from non-causal antecedents, plurality of causes, etc. The process of reasoning is discussed in detail and the analysis of the process remarkably resembles the syllogistic analysis of Aristotle. Some, for instance Max Müller, have considered this a coincidence, while others have treated it as an irrefutable proof of the Greeks borrowing from the Indians, or vice versa. In the absence of sufficient historical research on the subject, no very definite conclusion can be reached.

The first important exponent of the *Nyāya* was Gautama, who lived in the third century B.C. His *Nyāya Sūtra* is the first systematic exposition of its approach. The history of the

Nyāya is divided into two periods. The old *Nyāya* school ended with Gaṅgeśa (*c.* A.D. 1200) of Mithilā, the founder of the modern school. His *Tattvacintāmaṇi* is the standard text of the school in the second period. Partly inspired by the criticism of Śrīharsha, a member of the *Vedānta* school, who claimed that the *Nyāya* methods of dealing with knowledge of the external world were invalid and that it cannot really ever be proved whether a thing exists or not, Gaṅgeśa tried to build up a more rigorous structure for the discipline. There were various critics of the *Nyāya* school, but it is of interest to note that to debunk this discipline, the critics more often than not used the methods of reasoning of the *Nyāya* school. This really illustrates the importance of this school in Indian philosophical history.

The *Vaiśeshika* is more interested in cosmology. All material objects, it claims, are made of four kinds of atoms. Different combinations of these atoms of earth, water, fire, and air make different materials. But the substances of the world are not all material. There are in fact, it claims, nine substances; these include, apart from the four kinds of material atoms, space, time, ether (*ākāśa*), mind, and soul. It accepts a personal God. He created the world, but not out of nothing. The nine substances existed before the world was formed; He fashioned them into an ordered universe. God is thus the creator of the world, but not of its constituents. Therefore, the philosophy of the *Vaiśeshika*, while not atheistic, is different from that of most schools of traditional Hindu theology. In fact there were so many unorthodox thinkers in this school that Śaṃkara, the great champion of the *Vedānta*, described the followers of *Vaiśeshika* as *ardhavaināśikas*, i.e. half-nihilists.

The first notable member of the school was Kaṇāda (*c.* third century B.C.), whose *Vaiśeshika Sūtra* occupies in this sytem about the same place as the *Nyāya Sūtra* in the *Nyāya* school. Like the *Nyāya*, the *Vaiśeshika* too had two phases in its life. In fact the evolutions of the two systems have, throughout history, been very closely linked with each other. Together they represent the relatively analytical branch of Hindu philosophy.

The *Sāṃkhya* school was founded by Kapila, who lived probably in the seventh century B.C. The system is in one sense dualistic, since it recognizes two basic categories in the universe – the *purusha* and the *prakṛiti*. The *purusha* consists of selves or spirits, eternal entities of consciousness. The *prakṛiti* represents the potentiality of nature, the basis of all objective existence. It does not consist of matter alone and includes all resources of nature, material and psychical. The *prakṛiti* is thus the fundamental substance out of which, the *Sāṃkhya* claims, the world evolves. This evolution of the *prakṛiti* is possible only under the influence of the *purusha*, and the history of the world is the history of this evolution.

The *Sāṃkhya* believes very strongly in the principle of causation, and in fact uses this to show the necessity of assuming the eternal existence of *prakṛiti*, for something cannot come out of nothing. But, claims the *Sāṃkhya* school, while the cause and the effect are different things distinct from each other, the effect is always present in the cause. The former is just a different arrangement of the latter, both consisting of the same substance. A jar is *not* a lump of clay from which it is made, but they consist of the same substance. There is an underlying assumption of the indestructibility of substance. This view of causality has been strongly criticized by the *Nyayā-Vaiśeshika* school. A part of the difference between the two is verbal, but there is also a more real element in the difference between their respective views of causality and, hence, of evolution.

Another important *Sāṃkhya* contribution to Hindu thought is the doctrine of *triguṇa*, the three qualities of nature. The three qualities are *sattva* (light, purity, harmonious existence), *rajas* (energy, passion), and *tamas* (inertia, darkness). These three conflicting aspects of *prakṛiti* play different parts in its evolution. *Sattva* is primarily responsible for the manifestation of *prakṛiti* and the maintenance of its evolution. *Rajas* causes all activity and *tamas* is responsible for inertia and restraint. While these qualities conflict with each other, they all have their part in the evolution. Evolution proceeds through various stages. There is first the development of *buddhi* (intellect), described as the *mahat* (great). Then evolves the self-sense, the feeling of ego. Gradually develop the five cognitive organs, the five motor organs, and the disciplined mind.

For emancipation from the bondage of one's body, what is needed is the knowledge of the distinction between the *purusha* and the *prakṛiti*, the self and non-self. The self tends to confuse itself with *buddhi*, the intellect. When the knowledge of the distinction is achieved, the soul is no longer bound by the *prakṛiti*. The person becomes a disinterested spectator of the happenings in the world. At death the bond between the *purusha* and the *prakṛiti* is completely dissolved and the emancipated soul, unlike other souls, is free from rebirth. Bondage, according to this philosophy, is due to ignorance, and emancipation comes through knowledge.

The *Sāṃkhya* has been described as an atheistic philosophy, though this is not entirely correct. The *Sāṃkhya-pravacana Sūtra* (attributed to Kapila) finds it unnecessary to make the assumption of the existence of God, though it does not deny it either. It maintains that the existence of God cannot be *proved* by evidence. The later *Sāṃkhya* philosophers seem to abandon this agnostic position and the existence of God is later accepted. Vijñānabhikshu even tries to reconcile the *Sāṃkhya* views with those of the *Vedānta*.

The philosophical basis of the *Yoga* is the same as that of the *Sāṃkhya*, except that a personal God is introduced into the system. God controls the process of evolution and is, as one might expect, Omniscient and Omnipotent. Periodically He dissolves the cosmos and then initiates the process of evolution again.

In practice, the *Yoga* system of discipline consists of exercises of the mind and the body, including the very difficult exercise of not exercising them *at all*. In addition to making us healthier in mind and body in this world, these exercises are supposed to facilitate emancipation. Unlike the *Sāṃkhya* system, the *Yoga* school does not believe that freedom comes only from knowledge; the discipline of the mind and the body is supposed to contribute to the process. Various methods of concentration are recommended, as well as methods of suppressing those mental activities that increase our bondage by making us more dependent on *prakṛiti*. The *Yoga* system of exercises is still commonly practised in India. Apart from those seeking emancipation, there are those who find it a useful way of keeping their mind and body healthy. And there are of course those, including some from Europe, who have been attracted by its promise of prompt development of supernatural powers, a promise that, surprisingly, seems to have just as much appeal in this age as in any previous period in history.

We may now have a look at the last group, that of the *Pūrva-Mīmāṃsā* and the *Vedānta*. The main text of the first system is the *Pūrva-Mīmāṃsā Sūtra* by Jaimini (*c.* 400 B.C.). It is a scholastic piece of work and confines itself almost entirely to the interpretation of the *Vedas*. This school of philosophy is interested mainly in inquiring into the nature of *dharma* (right action), and since it accepts the *Vedas* to be both infallible and the sole authority on *dharma*, one can call it a fairly orthodox school. Its interest is more practical than speculative and its importance is less as a school of philosophy than as a useful system of interpreting the *Vedas*.

Perhaps the most influential of the philosophical systems has been, and still is, the *Vedānta*. It springs from the *Upanishads* and its central thesis is the Upanishadic doctrine of the *Brahman*. Its founder was Bādarāyaṇa, whose *Brahma Sūtra* (also called the *Uttar-Mīmāṃsā*) makes up, along with the *Upanishads* and the *Bhagavad-Gītā*, the foundation of the *Vedānta* system. The most famous exponent of the *Vedānta* was undoubtedly Śaṃkara, who lived in South India in the eighth century A.D. There are two main divisions in the *Vedānta* school, one rigidly non-dualistic (*advaita*) in its outlook and the other tolerating various degrees of dualism (*dvaita*). Śaṃkara was the champion of the former branch of the school.

Śaṃkara was preceded by Gauḍapāda, a believer in a very strict form of monism. He asserted categorically that the external world was unreal, the only reality being the *Brahman*. Outer objects are purely subjective, and dreams are hardly different from our experiences while we are awake. The whole world is a vast illusion and nothing exists other than the *Brahman*. Like the Buddhist spiritual absolutist Nāgārjuna, Gauḍapāda denies the possibility of change or the validity of causation. 'There is no destruction, no creation, none in bondage, none endeavouring [for release], none desirous of liberation, none liberated; this is the absolute truth.'

Śaṃkara's position is less extreme. While asserting the identity of the *Brahman* with the *Ātman*, and denying that the world was outside the Supreme, he did not accept the description of the world as a pure illusion. Waking experiences are different from dreams and external objects are not merely forms of personal consciousness. Śaṃkara explains the appearance of the world with an analogy. A person may mistake a rope for a serpent. The serpent is not there, but it is not entirely an illusion, for there is the rope. The appearance of the serpent lasts until the rope is closely examined. The world can be compared with the serpent and the *Brahman* with the rope. When we acquire true knowledge we recognize that the world is only a manifestation of the *Brahman*. The world is neither real nor quite unreal; it is an appearance based on the existence of the *Brahman*. The precise relationship between the *Brahman* and the world is inexpressible and is sometimes referred to as *māyā*.

Statements about *Brahman*, to be intelligible, must use empirical forms. The wise recognize these forms to be necessities of concrete thought, but fools take them to be the real truth. One must also recognize that the relationship between the *Brahman* and the world is not reversible. There will be no world without the *Brahman*, but the existence of the *Brahman* does not depend on the appearance of the world, just as the appearance of the serpent depends on the existence of the rope but not vice versa.

The *jīva*, or the individual soul, is a particular manifestation of the *Brahman*. Because of *avidyā* (ignorance), the root of all troubles, the ego-feeling exists. The end is liberation, and that is achieved through a practical realization (not merely a theoretical acceptance) of the oneness of the self with the Absolute. If a person reaches this state he becomes *jīvan-mukta*, i.e. liberated while alive. Realizing the oneness of all, his life becomes one of unselfish service. At death his freedom from bondage is complete. Casting off the physical body, the soul becomes completely free.

Somewhat different interpretations of the *Upanishads* were put forward by some later Vedāntists. Two *Vaishṇava* scholars, Rāmānuja and Madhva, were prominent among the branch of the *Vedānta* that is sometimes called dualistic (*dvaita*). Rāmānuja's philosophy was in fact a different version of the *advaita* doctrine. To put it in a few words, he claimed that the world, the *Ātman* and God (*Īśvara*) are distinct though not separate. The individual souls and the concrete world are like the body of God, and *Īśvara* possessed of the two is the *Brahman*. Thus, everything is within the *Brahman*, but still individual souls are different from *Īśvara*. The thesis, as we shall see later, helped the intellectual acceptance of the *Bhakti* movement, i.e. the approach to God through devotion rather than through knowledge.

Rāmānuja belonged to the eleventh century. Madhva came in the thirteenth. He believed in the dualism of the *Brahman* and the *jīva* (the individual souls). His philosophy is, thus, called *Dvaita*. In fact he also accepted the existence of the physical world, thereby introducing a third entity. *Brahman*, or God (*Vishṇu*), is of course complete, perfect, and the highest reality, but the world too is real. The differences between Śaṃkara's philosophy and that of Madhva can be readily noticed. The *Vaishṇava* movement, as one might imagine, owed much to the contribution of Madhva.

We have presented above a brief, and consequently extremely incomplete, account of the main systems of Hindu philosophy. One can notice wide variations between the theses of the different schools. We find among them monism, dualism, and pantheism, even complete agnosticism. Some claim that the world was created by God out of nothing. Others maintain that substances existed always and God only refashioned them to make an ordered universe. Others find the development of the world and of life as a process of evolution of nature under the influence of *purusha* (selves) without any necessary presence of God. Still others find that the world is not quite real, being only an aspect of God, and there is no real creation at all. Different religious leaders have belonged to different schools, and most Hindus are rather proud of the fact that there have not been any violent conflicts or persecution, thanks to mutual tolerance. This is a field where no one theory can claim to explain all the mysteries, and tolerance may well be the path to wisdom rather than that to confusion.

CHAPTER 16

Hinduism Outside India

THE spread of Hindu religion and culture to south-east Asia began about the middle of the first millennium B.C. India had, from very early days, developed extensive mercantile contacts with Java, Sumatra, Cambodia, Burma, Malaya, Thailand, and other countries of the region. Partly through these trading contacts, partly through political conquests, but also through emigration of Indian colonists, Hindu culture spread to this area of the world.

The *Rāmāyaṇa* refers to contacts with Suvarṇa-dvīpa (Sanskrit, 'Gold-island') and Yava-dvīpa (Sanskrit, 'Barley-island') in south-east Asia. The precise geographical areas referred to by these names are difficult to identify, but the latter probably refers to Java and the former to Sumatra and the Malayan Peninsula. The *Purāṇas* also mention Malaya-dvīpa. Chinese dynastic chronicles mention that in the first century A.D. a Hindu kingdom (called Funan) was founded in Cambodia by a Brahmin named Kauṇḍinya. The Chinese also record that Hindu states existed in the Malayan Peninsula from the second century A.D. In the same century Chinese accounts mention the state of Campā (as the kingdom of Lin-yi) situated along the coast of Indo-China above Cambodia. Sanskrit inscriptions from before A.D. 400 show that the state of Campā was Indianized with a Hindu ruler. In Thailand the earliest Indianized material unearthed so far are some small bronze statues of the Buddha in the Amarāvatī style which flourished in India between the second and the fourth centuries A.D. Burmese chronicles relate that in the third century B.C. the Indian emperor Aśoka sent Buddhist missionaries to Burma. Some historians have doubted the authenticity of this record, but there is no doubt that India's contact with Burma started very early.

The political importance of different areas in south-east

Asia changed in the course of time. In the first few centuries of the Christian era the Indianized kingdom of Funan (Cambodia) was the most powerful state in the area. After its decline the kingdom of Śrīvijaya in Sumatra became prominent. In the eighth century A.D. a Hindu king, Sañjaya, founded a powerful state in Java. Later in the century this was replaced by a Buddhist dynasty, the Śailendras, who installed themselves as the Mahārājās of Śrīvijaya and controlled a vast empire. From the ninth century A.D., however, Hindu kingdoms revived in Java. The kingdom of Mataram was defeated in early eleventh century by Śrīvijava, but it revived again later in the century. By the fourteenth century the Hindu kingdom of Majapahit in Eastern Java had achieved considerable importance.

In Cambodia the Khmer kingdom conquered Funan in the sixth century. For some time the Khmers were to some extent under Śailendra influence, but they recovered in the ninth century under the leadership of Jayavarmaṇa II, who founded the Angkor dynasty. This was largely Hindu, though *Mahāyāna* Buddhism also had a following.

In Burma it was largely through the *Mon* people of Lower Burma that the Indian influence spread. The most powerful Burmese empire was the Pagan kingdom which was Buddhist. Its great king Anuratha lived in the eleventh century, and the kingdom was destroyed by Mongol invasion in the fourteenth century.

From the thirteenth century onwards Islamic influence grew in south-east Asia, and soon Java, Sumatra, and some other countries in the region took to the new faith. Interestingly enough, Islam like Hinduism and Buddhism also came to this region from India. As Professor Brian Harrison remarks:

> Persian and Arab merchants continued to visit its ports during all that time [seven hundred years from the foundation of Islam], and knowledge of Islam came with them, but it was not until the faith was presented by Indian Moslems that it became acceptable. It was not to Persia or Arabia but to India that south-east Asia had always looked for cultural inspiration combined with commercial

prestige. The acceptance of Islam among the islands and in the Malay peninsula had therefore to await its acceptance by Indians who were prominently engaged in the overseas trade between India and south-east Asia. It was not until the thirteenth century that this condition was fulfilled. . . .[1]

It was mainly through the Gujrati mercantile community that Islamic influence spread in the region. However, some parts of the area remained Hindu (e.g. Bali), and Buddhism, of course, continued to flourish in Burma, Indo-China, and Thailand. Even in the regions converted to Islam, Hindu and Buddhist culture continued to live through art, literature, mythology, and, to some extent, in the mode of life.

In studying the contribution of Hinduism to south-east Asia we must examine not merely the religious beliefs and practices introduced by the Hindus but also the influence that Hindu literature, sculpture, architecture, and the Sanskrit language had on the culture of the area. In most of these countries the art of writing came with the Hindus, their scripts being based mainly on North Indian or South Indian letters. The vocabulary of their languages was vastly enriched by the inclusion of Sanskrit (or Pāli) words, as is clear from a study of their philology. This Sanskrit influence was of course intimately connected with religion, for one of the main reasons for studying Sanskrit or Pāli was the desire to read Hindu and Buddhist scriptures. The study of Sanskrit literature, which included non-religious literature, was partly a by-product of this desire.

The influences of Indian Hindu and Buddhist architecture and sculpture on the art of these countries is well-known. The majestic and beautiful temples of Borobodur, Lara-Jongrang, Angkor Vat, and Ananda are examples of this, for the sculptures are images of gods in the Indian mythology.

As for the forms of Hinduism, the worship of God as the all-powerful Śiva seems to have been common in most parts, though Vishṇu was more prominent during some dynasties. The main temple of Lara-Jongrang in Java was dedicated

1. *South-east Asia*. London, 1954, p. 43.

to Śiva, but the magnificent Angkor Vat is a Vaishṇavite product. There has been no conflict between Buddhism and Hinduism, and quite a number of temples contain images of Buddha and figures from Hindu mythology. In this period Hinduism and Buddhism existed side by side without any violent crusade even in India, and this process of compromise and assimilation can be observed in south-east Asia also.

In discussing the Indian influence on south-east Asia, it must not be forgotten, as it unfortunately sometimes is, that it was the native genius of this region that made possible the flowering of such a great culture. The inspiration was Hindu or Buddhist, the techniques initially were Indian, but it was the talent of the population of the whole area that made the culture as rich as it was. For example, although early Khmer art followed Indian traditions very closely, in the Angkor period it evolved a style that was quite distinct from anything produced in India. Similarly the Hindu religious beliefs in this area were somewhat different from the main current of Indian Hindu thought. In Central Java, for example, the cult of Agastya was quite common. Agastya is an Indian figure and is looked upon, in Indian mythology, as a great sage, but in Java he seems to have acquired a divinity which he did not enjoy in India. In this connexion it may also be worthwhile mentioning that some of the south-east Asian Hindu kings succeeded in making themselves more divine than their counterparts in India managed to do. Similarly the Śiva-Buddha cult of thirteenth-century Java, while somewhat akin to the *Tāntrik* Buddhist cult in India, was a distinct religious school.

In scholarship and academic pursuits south-east Asia made considerable contributions. Many scholars went to India (especially to the Nālandā University in East Bihar) for studies, particularly in the early periods, but at the same time some of the centres of learning in south-east Asia were so good that students from India and other foreign countries went there to work. The famous Chinese Buddhist pilgrim I-tsing, who visited Śrīvijaya in Sumatra in A.D. 671 on his way to India, spent six months in Śrīvijaya studying

Sanskrit grammar. Dīpaṅkara Srījñāna, also known as Atīśa, the great Indian Buddhist scholar who reformed Tibetan Buddhism, is said to have studied in Śrīvijaya from 1011 to 1023 under Dharmakīrti, the head of the clergy in Sumatra. Thus the Hindu and Buddhist achievements in south-east Asia should not be looked upon as purely Indian contributions, but as basically south-east Asian achievements built on Hindu or Buddhist inspiration.

In this context it is interesting to compare the contribution of Hinduism to Far Eastern Buddhism with its effect on south-east Asian culture. In relation to Chinese or Japanese Buddhism, the role of the Hindus is similar to that of the Jews in relation to Christianity: they gave birth to it but did not (in the long run, in the case of the Indians) accept it. In relation to south-east Asia, however, India's role is more similar to that of Greece and Rome *vis-à-vis* Western culture. It provided the techniques and basis of inspiration on which a flourishing culture was developed by the native genius of south-east Asia.

CHAPTER 17

Bhakti or the Devotional School

Of the three Hindu religious paths, *jñāna*, the path of knowledge, is apt to be dry and hard, and *karma*, the path of work (of religious performances), has often been exclusive. It is not surprising therefore that *bhakti*, the path of devotion, has enjoyed great popularity. The religious expression of this cult is in love and adoration, and it implies a belief in the Supreme Person rather than in a Supreme Abstraction. Naturally this school of thought has not been much concerned with the intricacies of theology, and compared with the teachings of the *Upanishads*, the *Sāṃkhya*, or the *Advaita Vedānta*, is less sophisticated. God is here looked upon as an intensely lovable Creator, and the *Bhakti* movement led to religious exuberance rather than to calm speculations about the all-pervading *Brahman*.

The *Bhakti* movement centred mainly around the deities Vishṇu and Śiva. Śiva seems to be of non-Aryan origin.[1] There are some, though relatively few, hymns to Vishṇu in the *Vedas*, but it is believed that his popularity, too, may have been due to his identification with some non-Aryan deity. The *Bhakti* movement seems therefore to have non-Aryan roots, and indeed the *Padmapurāna* declares *Bhakti* to be a product of the Dravidian land. There is no doubt that the *Bhakti* movement was long opposed by Brahmins, because its disregard of traditional religious ceremonies and its indifference to caste divisions annoyed the Brahmins. Later, however, when the movement itself became relatively more orthodox. Brahmins took to it in large numbers.

1. Like most other propositions about ancient Indian history, this too may be questionable. See, for example, 'An Historical Sketch of Śaivism' by K. A. Nilakanta Sastri, in *The Cultural Heritage of India*. Ramakrishna Centenary Committee, Volume II. Calcutta, pp. 20–3. Pandit Nilakanta Sastri doubts the proposition that Śaivism is pre-Vedic and non-Aryan in origin. He accepts, however, that there are considerable non-Aryan elements in Śaivism.

In the *Mahābhārata* there are references to *Vaishṇava* sects (devotees of Vishṇu), so the *Vaishṇava* movement must be fairly old. In the second century B.C. we also hear of a Greek devotee of Vishṇu, Heliodorus. Kṛishṇa of the *Bhagavad-Gītā* is looked upon as an incarnation of Vishṇu. The worship of Kṛishṇa (literal meaning, black) may at first have been confined to the *Ābhīra* tribe, who seem to have led a nomadic life between Mathurā and Dvārakā. There are so many legendary folk-stories associated with Kṛishṇa that it is highly probable that his origins are to be found in some popular deity. Later Kṛishṇa, Vishṇu, and Nārāyaṇa all seem to merge into one god. Later still Vishṇu becomes, to one school of devotees, synonymous with the Supreme, just as Śiva does to another school. The doctrine of *Pañcarātra*, with its emphasis on devotion, is a branch of Vaishṇavism which accepts the idea of many incarnations of Vishṇu. Kṛishṇa, of course, is the incarnation that is best-known, but Rāma of the *Rāmāyaṇa* is also accepted as an incarnation, and in Purānic accounts ten incarnations are mentioned, which include Buddha. The rise of Vishṇu from an unacceptable non-Aryan god to the position of the absolute Supreme, with Rāma and Kṛishṇa, and even Buddha, as his incarnations, is an interesting story of mythological evolution.

In South India, among the Tamils, there is a long and ancient tradition of *bhakti* in the works of the *Ālvār* saints. It has been claimed that the earliest of them belonged to pre-Vedic times, which is very doubtful, but the tradition is certainly quite old. The last of them are found about the eighth or the ninth centuries A.D. Most of these *Ālvār* saints came from low castes, and the movement may have been restricted for some time to the lower strata of the society, who got little from the orthodox Brahminical Hinduism. Later *Vaishṇavas* of even higher castes were forced to accept their literature, such as *Tiru Vāymoli*, as religious works of great significance, and Rāmānuja recognized their works as the *Veda* of the *Vaishṇavas*. One of the *Ālvārs*, Anḍāl, was a woman of low caste, and the fact that she was accepted later as a religious leader in a caste-ridden male-dominated society is greatly to the credit of the *Bhakti* movement. From the tradition of the *Ālvārs*, through their followers, like Nāthamuni, Alvandar-Yāmunācārya, and Pilley-Lokācārya (the author of the *Arthapañcaka*, 1213), the *Bhakti* movement gradually developed till it found eloquent expression in the works of Rāmānuja.

Ālvār prayers are simple and full of the religious devotion traditional in the *Bhakti* school. 'Lord, we have no strength by which we can know you. May our lives never be deflected from you.' Later *Bhakti* philosophers, like Nāthamuni and Yāmunācārya, were more sophisticated and seemed to have lacked the utter simplicity of the *Ālvārs*. Rāmānuja was, of course, a great scholar and he provided the *Bhakti* movement with an intellectual basis. Unlike the *Vedānta* school of Śaṃkara, Rāmānuja looked upon individual souls as distinct and different from God, and his approach is, as we have mentioned earlier, rather different from that of the pure *Advaita* school. He was also less concerned with knowledge than with devotion, and put forward the point of view that the main trouble was not 'ignorance', but unbelief.

The *Vaishṇava Bhakti* movement also grew in other parts of the country besides South India. The devotional songs of *Mīrā Bāi* (*c.* 1504), the Rajput woman devotee, are well-known. Their popularity does not seem to have diminished at all in four and a half centuries, and even today Mīrā's songs are very commonly sung. In the Mahārāshṭra we find Nāmadeva and Tukārāma, who were called *vitthala* and were worshippers of Vishṇu. Nāmadeva was probably born in the fourteenth century and was a tailor. We also hear of Nāmadeva's teacher who told Nāmadeva: 'The stone image speaks not, see the Lord within. The *tīrthas* [places of pilgrimage] cannot wash away sins; clean your heart instead. Fasting and other observances are futile unless your being is purified. What can ceremonies do if love awake not in your heart?' Nāmadeva also believed in the simple, direct approach to God of the *Bhakti* school. He sang, 'It is the one Lord who contains all. O Lord, why this vain seeking for you, since you are everywhere?'

Tukārāma probably lived in the seventeenth century. He

came from a poor peasant family. 'O thou great One,' he sang, 'Thy majesty is beyond all description. How shall I hymn thee? Let Thy grace protect us.' 'My enemies are not in the world outside. It is the passions within me that bring dangers and difficulties. Who but Thou can save us from their attacks?'

Another centre of the *Vaishṇava Bhakti* movement was Mathurā, where the school founded by Vallabhācārya flourished. From there the movement spread to other parts of the country like Rajputana and Punjab. Among the followers of Vallabhācārya was Vilvamaṅgala of Karṇāta, probably born in the fifteenth century, whose book *Kṛishṇa-karṇāmṛita* is a masterpiece of devotional writing.

In Bengal the best-known figure in the *Bhakti* movement is Caitanya (1485–1533). Before his time the people of Bengal had been influenced by the *Vaishṇava* poets Jayadeva, Vidyāpati, and Caṇḍīdās, but it was Caitanya who revived the *Bhakti* cult into a powerful religious movement which, true to the *Bhakti* tradition, produced a rich flow of devotional poems and songs. In Assam there was a *Vaishṇava Bhakti* movement in the sixteenth century led by Śaṃkaradeva. There were many other *Vaishṇava* movements in various parts of the country, and although we cannot discuss all of them here, it should now be clear how widespread the *Vaishṇava Bhakti* movement was. It may be mentioned, however, that in spite of the unorthodox nature of the movement it could not always break through all caste-barriers. It is true that many leaders of the cult came from the lower castes, particularly at the early stages of the *Bhakti* movements, and that most *Vaishṇava Bhakti* literature reveals a belief in the equality of men, but there can be no doubt that considerable elements of caste-distinction remained within the movement. Rāmānuja accepted caste-divisions in some limited form, and even Caitanya failed to do away with them completely. Thus, in spite of a tendency towards liberalization, the movement did not achieve as much equality of status as is sometimes claimed. It must also be admitted that in some branches of the movement, devotees seem to have taken love and adoration in their more literal and human sense, and that in these cases the moral conduct of the devotees often left much to be desired.

The *Śaiva* movement was less widespread than the *Vaishṇava* cult, though its following was by no means negligible. Śiva, as we have mentioned earlier, was at first a non-Aryan god, to whose worship the Brahmins were opposed. Gradually, however, Śiva came to be accepted. Towards the end of the sixth century we find an injunction by Varāhamihira that only Brahmins may act as priests in the *Śaiva* temples. This proves acceptance of the deity, but Brahmin priests of *Śaiva* temples seem to have had a somewhat lower social status. From *Śiva-jñāna-bodham* (1223) we learn that most of the *Śaiva bhaktas* were non-Brahmins. There followed a long line of *Śaiva* devotees, and we find Sivavākya, in the seventeenth century, asking: 'What can be done by these artificial gods whose honour and even existence are under human control? How can they bring salvation to me? What is the use, then, of arranging flowers near a block of stone, and what benefit accrues from the burning of incense, and the sounding of bells before an idol, and from circumambulating it and observing similar other practices? In the same way, vain is the observance of ninety-six rules by the *Yogī* and the incarceration of the flesh, the muttering of *mantras*, pilgrimage to holy places, and bathing in the Ganges. So give up attachment and pacify the mind; the holy Banaras will rise up in your heart. It is the ideal Divinity and not the artificial images that is to be worshipped.' Bhadira-giriar put this *Bhakti* thought into the simple verse: 'When, O Lord, will my senses be curbed, my pride turned down, my struggles be ended in an excellent repose?' 'When will freedom come to me who am like an imprisoned fish, and when shall I be able to lay myself at the feet of God and merge my own nature into His?'

In Kashmir also the *Śaiva Bhakti* movement was strong. The most famous Kashmiri expositor of *Śaiva* philosophy was Abhinavagupta, who lived in the eleventh century. Among his predecessors, Siddha Somānanda is well-known. Their works were sometimes too intellectual for ordinary devotees and many *bhaktas* had simple devotional songs free from theological speculation.

An interesting offshoot of the *Śaiva* cult was the *Viraśaiva* or *Liṅgāyata*, which appeared in Karṇāṭaka in the twelfth century. It too was unorthodox in its approach, though the *guru* of the school came from Brahmin stock. It emphasized devotion and faith, and opposed priest-ridden ritualism.

We have not been able to cover all the different forms of *Bhakti* movement. Because of its very nature it had great appeal to religiously-minded people at different places and in different ages. In addition to the *Bhakti* movements centred around Vishṇu and Śiva, there are others devoted to other forms of God. Some worshipped the Supreme as Devī – a development from the cult of the mother-goddess found in pre-Aryan days. The worshippers of the mother-goddess are sometimes called *Śāktas*, from Śakti, another name for Devī, Kālī, or Durgā. This branch of the *Bhakti* movement has been connected with the *Tantras*, which we discussed in Chapter 13. There can be no doubt, however, that of the different *Bhakti* schools the *Vaishṇavas* and the *Śaivas* were the most prominent. It is along these two streams that the devotional impulse of the Hindu *bhaktas* has mainly flown.

CHAPTER 18

Medieval Mysticism of North India

INDIAN culture represents the combined achievement of many races and communities. The coming of Islam to India led to a series of remarkable responses. Their passionate concern with the present has led many Indians to ignore these influences, but an objective study of the evolution of Hindu tradition must take into account the creative influence of this great religion.

It is impossible for two cultures to exist side by side without influencing one another, and in India the Hindu and Muslim patterns of culture have had a good deal of intercourse. Evidence for this can be found not only in the development of new schools of painting (e.g. Moghul, Rajput, Kangra, Gharwal), sculpture and architecture (e.g. that of the Tājmahal), and music (influencing the trend of Indian classical music), it can also be observed in religious movements. Indeed the devotional movement of the *Bhakti* cult and the tradition of the Islamic *Sūfis* have so much in common that intercourse was easy. The product of the meeting of these two schools was the strangely attractive North Indian medieval mysticism. The word medieval is perhaps a misleading one, for in most minds it is associated with the ideas and practices of the Middle Ages in Europe, whereas the movement we are considering is almost entirely different. The outstanding aspect of Indian medieval mysticism is its complete independence from sectarian organizations and orthodox scriptures.

The story of Islamic influence may perhaps be said to start with Makhdūm Saiyad Ali al Hujwiri, who died in A.D. 1072, but the first *Sūfi* teacher to come to India was Khwājā Moinuddin Cishti, who was born in Seistān in 1142. He arrived at Delhi in 1193 and finally settled down in Pushkar, a place of Hindu pilgrimage in Ajmer. He had many disciples, both Muslim and Hindu. The present writer was amused to meet in Pushkar a class of people, followers of Cishti, who call themselves 'Husaini Brahmins'. In the following centuries there were numerous *Sūfi* teachers in India, but we cannot discuss the movement here except in so far as it influenced Hindu thought.[1]

On the Hindu side the man who gave medieval mysticism its momentum was Rāmānanda (*c.* 1370–1440). He started as a follower of Rāmānuja, but moved away from the orthodoxy of the movement. He challenged caste-divisions, questioned the traditional religious ceremonies, and by preaching in Hindi rather than in Sanskrit, which was confined to the upper classes, gave an impetus to popular literature. He accepted all that he found good in Hindu religion – its philosophy of knowledge (*jñāna*) and meditation (*yoga*), its tradition of devotion (*bhakti*) – but because he was not bound by the orthodox customs of the traditional Hindus, he could give his religious movement much greater popular appeal. The nature of his thought is well reflected in one of his poems to be found in the Sikh anthology, *Granth Sāheb*: 'Wherever I go, I see water and stone (made the medium of worship); but it is You who had filled them all with Your presence. In vain do they seek You in the *Vedas*. . . . My own true *Guru*, You have put an end to all my failures and illusions. Blessed are You. Rāmānanda is lost in his Master, *Brahman*; it is the *Guru*'s word that breaks all bonds.'

Rāmānanda is supposed to have had twelve principal disciples, most of whom came from low castes. One of them, Ravidās, was a cobbler. More than thirty of his devotional songs are included in the *Granth Sāheb*. 'The recitation of the Vedic *mantras*,' he sang, 'even for many millions of times, will not satisfy the pangs of that longing. In every object You are existing all the while. It is my fault that I have not learnt to see You with my own eyes.'

By far the most famous of Rāmānanda's disciples was a Muslim weaver, Kabīr. The exact dates of his birth and

1. The interested reader may find some material on this in my book *Medieval Mysticism of India*, London, 1936, pp. 14–41. Most of the verses quoted in this and the previous chapter are reproduced from this book.

death are uncertain and there are conflicting theories about them. However, in all probability he lived mainly in the fifteenth century and may even have been a *direct* disciple of Rāmānanda. The son of a Muslim weaver, converted to the movement, he struck at the roots of every kind of religious ritualism and superstition. He combined in him the *Sūfi* and *Bhakti* traditions of the Islamic and the Hindu religion. 'O God, whether Allah or Rāma, I live by Thy Name,' sang Kabīr. 'The difference among faiths is only one in names; everywhere the yearning is for the same God.' Kabīr composed songs for the common people, and naturally chose Hindi rather than Sanskrit as his medium. 'Sanskrit is like water in a well,' said Kabīr, 'the language of the people is a flowing stream.' He did not believe in austerity or celibacy. He was married, had a son and a daughter, and continued his life as a craftsman. In the life of this illiterate weaver there was indeed a rare balance of material and spiritual values. 'By saying that the Supreme Reality only dwells in the inner realm of spirit, we shame the outer world of matter; and also when we say that He is only in the outside, we do not speak the truth.'

Kabīr had many followers both among the Hindus and the Muslims. There is a charming legend about a quarrel between the Hindus and the Muslims after his death, both sects wishing to have a funeral of their own sort. According to the legend, when the shroud was removed, they found not Kabīr's body, but bunches of flowers, which were divided equally between the contending parties. After Kabīr's death his son Kamāl was asked by some to organize a sect of his father's followers. Kamāl rejected the idea and pointed out that his father had fought throughout his life against all forms of sectarianism and that to organize such a sect would be to contradict the spirit of Kabīr's religious faith. However, some of Kabīr's disciples – mostly Muslims – built a monastery on Kabīr's tomb in Magahar, while the Hindu disciples had a centre at Banaras and another at Chattisgarh. Of these the latter sect is the bigger, and is believed to have some four million members. The founder of the great Sikh religion, Nānak (1469–1538), was greatly influenced by

Kabīr's teaching, which was known as *Kabīrpanth*. Some of the attractive simplicity of Sikhism can be traced to Kabīr and the Sikh religious document *Granth Sāheb* is an important source of medieval mystical verses.

Outstanding among Kabīr's followers was Dādu (1544–1603), a cotton-carder who came from a Muslim family. There have been some attempts by some of his later followers to show that he came from a Brahmin family, just as in *Bhaktamāla*, a sixteenth-century Hindu document on the *Bhakti* movement, Kabīr's descent from a Muslim family is concealed. Not only are these assertions of the orthodox devotees of Kabīr and Dādu incorrect; they also reflect a strange view of the teachings of their masters. One of Dādu's dreams was the unification of faiths, and it was with this object that he founded the *Brahma-Sampradāya* for the worship of God without ritual or orthodoxy. Dādu described the essence of the *Brahma* Society as 'The giving up of self-regard, the worship of God, the curing of all corruptions of mind and body, the cultivation of friendliness for all creatures – that is its essence.' This is not very different from the teaching of the *Bhagavad-Gītā*, but its approach is perhaps more direct, and free from the grand metaphysics of the *Gītā*. Dādu once described his ancestry: 'God is my forebear, the Creator is my kinsman, the world-*guru* is of my caste, I belong to the children of the Almighty.' It is this simplicity of faith and this confidence in knowing God, coupled with his liberal outlook, that attracted Akbar, the Great Moghul. The emperor had a long religious discussion with Dādu lasting over forty days and is supposed to have been strongly influenced by Dādu's teaching. Akbar himself later began an attempt to unite all religious faiths in his *Dīn-i-Ilāhi*, and in all probability it was Dādu's *Brahma-Sampradāya* that helped him to such a liberal outlook.

The theme of many of Dādu's poems is the beauty of the world. He did not believe in asceticism and he pointed out that, in creating the senses, God did not intend them to be starved. 'And so,' says Dādu, 'the eye is feasted with colour, the ear with music, the palate with flavours, wondrously provided.'

'When I look upon the beauty of this Universe,' sang Dādu, 'I cannot help asking: "How, O Lord, did You come to create it? What sudden wave of joy coursing through Your being compelled its own manifestation? Was it really due to a desire for self-expression, or simply on the impulse of emotion? Or was it perhaps just Your fancy to revel in the play of form? Is this play then so delightful to You? Or is it that You would see Your inborn delight thus take shape? Oh, how can these questions be answered in words; only those who know will understand."

'That is why Your Universe, this creation of Yours, has charmed me so – Your waters and Your breezes, and this earth which holds them, with its ranges of mountains, its great oceans, its snow-capped poles, its blazing sun, because, through all the three regions of earth, sky, and heavens, amidst all their multifarious life, it is Your ministration, Your beauty, that keeps me enthralled. Who can know You, O Invisible, Unapproachable, Unfathomable? Dādu has no desire to know; he is satisfied to remain enraptured with all this beauty of Yours, and to rejoice in it with You.'

This is *bhakti* in its purest form – strikingly different from the intellectual 'path of knowledge' (*jñāna*) and the complicated 'path of work' (*karma*). This tradition was carried on after Dādu's death by many of his followers, of whom most famous was Rajjab. 'All this world', said Rajjab, 'is the *Vedas* and the entire creation is the *Korān*. Vain are efforts of the Pandit and the Kāzi who consider a mass of dry papers to be their complete world.' 'There are as many sects as there are men. Such is the creation of Providence endowed with a variety. The worship of different sects, which are like so many small streams, move together to meet Hari (God), who is like the ocean.'

There were many medieval mystics who contributed to this tradition of devotional songs, but we cannot discuss all of them in this short book. Some of them, like the sixteenth-century Hindi poet Tulasīdāsa who translated the *Rāmāyaṇa* from Sanskrit to Hindi, are well-known. Others, like Dharaṇīdāsa, are not so well remembered except in particular areas. The common characteristic of all of them is their worship of God as a loving and intensely lovable Creator.

The medieval mysticism of one part of India – Sind – however, deserves special study, for there the influence of the Muslim *Sūfi* tradition was much stronger than that of the *Bhakti* school. The difference is not enormous, as the two traditions have much in common, but the words and the symbolism used tend to be different. Just as in the medieval mysticism of other areas the *Bhakti* tradition was influenced by *Sūfi* thought, so here the *Sūfi* tradition did not remain uninfluenced by *Bhakti* thought. The seventeenth century gave the movement Shāh Karīṃ and Shāh Inayet; Shāh Latīf was born in 1689; and this tradition has continued to the present day.

Closely connected with this school were the neo-*Sūfis* of Delhi. In the seventeenth century there was a *Sūfi* in Delhi called Bāwri Sāheb, whose disciple Bīru Sāheb was Hindu by birth. The latter, in turn, had a disciple called Yāṛi Shāh, who was Muslim by birth. Yāri Shāh's writings sometimes refer to the Divine as Āllah and sometimes as Rāma or Hari. All this may perhaps illustrate the extent to which Hindu and Muslim mysticism influenced each other.

CHAPTER 19

The Bāuls

THE religious life of India has produced few more interesting phenomena than the *Bāuls* of Bengal. Little known outside the province and without much honour even there, they provide a most moving example of the 'simple' (*sahaj*) man's search for 'the Man of my heart' (*moner mānush*), which is how they refer to Him. *Bāul* means madcap and is probably derived from the Sanskrit word *vāyu* (wind) in its sense of nerve currents. Another derivation connects it with the regulated breathing exercises which are practised by some cults. The religious tradition grew on the ruins of Buddhism, *Tantra*, and Vaishṇavism, and whatever the origin of their name the *Bāuls* are indeed true to it. Ever on the move, removed from all traditional ties, the *Bāuls* are free as the wind.

The main features of the *Bāul* movement are well expressed in the following song of Narahari Bāul:

That is why, brother, I became a madcap *Bāul*.
No master I obey, nor injunctions, canons, or custom.
Man-made distinctions have no hold on me now.
I rejoice in the gladness of the love that wells out of my own being.
In love there is no separation, but a meeting of hearts forever.
So I rejoice in song and I dance with each and all.
That is why, brother, I became a madcap *Bāul*.

These lines also introduce some of the main tenets of the *Bāul* cult. The freedom which the *Bāul* seeks is freedom from all outward compulsions. To be free one must die to the life of the world even while one is in it. This is sometimes called *fanā*, a word often used by *Sūfi* saints and mystics. The membership of the movement includes householders as well as vagrant wanderers. The *Bāuls* accept no divisions of society, such as caste or class, no special deity, nor any temple or mosque. They sometimes congregate during religious festivals, mainly those of the *Vaishṇavas*, but they do not take part in worship. Their ideal is to be *sahaj* (simple, natural) and they avoid and criticize the external forms of religious worship. As a rule the *Bāul* devotees come from the lowest social strata of the Hindu and the Muslim fold, and this is one of the reasons why they are often looked down upon by the orthodox members of both communities. Their general attitude towards temples and mosques, as well as other forms of religious institutions, may have had its origin in the restrictions operating against their low-caste brethren. 'What need have we of other temples,' they ask, 'when our body is the temple where our Spirit has its abode?' 'The devotee has within him the scroll on which the scriptures are written in letters of life; but, alas, few care to read them; men turn a deaf ear to the message of the heart.' The *Bāuls* also refuse to wear the ochre-coloured garb of the Indian hermits and monks. Their reply to this show of formalism is:

Can the colour show outside, unless the inside is tinctured first?
Does the fruit grow ripe and sweet by the painting of its skin?

It is difficult to trace the origin of the *Bāul* movement, for there are no written records, largely because the movement has been confined to members of the lowest strata of society, who are more often than not illiterate. Another reason, however, is their prejudice against recording their history. I remember once in a village in East Bengal I was conversing with a *Bāul* seated on the river bank. 'Why is it', I asked him, 'that you keep no historical record of yourself for the use of posterity?' 'We follow the *sahaj* [simple] way,' he replied, 'and so leave no trace behind us.' The tide had then ebbed, and there was little water in the river bed. Only a few boatmen could be seen pushing their boats along the mud, leaving long grooves behind them. 'Do the boats', the *Bāul* continued, 'that sail over the flooded river leave any mark? It is only the boatmen of the muddy track, urged on by their petty needs, that leave a long furrow behind. This is not the *sahaj* way. The true endeavour is to keep oneself afloat in the stream of devotion that flows through the lives of the devotees, and to mingle one's own devotion with theirs. There are many classes of men amongst the *Bāuls*, but they are all just *Bāuls*; they have no other achievement or history. All the streams that fall into the Ganges become the Ganges.' When I asked why they do not recognize the scriptures, another *Bāul*, obviously slightly irritated by the question, replied, 'Are we dogs that we should lick up the leavings of the others? Brave men rejoice in their own creation. Only the cowards are content with glorifying their forefathers because they do not know how to create for themselves.' The *Bāuls* have never bothered about the history of their sect. They are not concerned with what men have done or thought in the past, but only with their own devotional feelings today. The same attitude is responsible for their opposition to the pilgrimages. They sing:

I would not go, my heart, to Mecca or Medina,
For, behold, I ever abide by the side of my Friend.
Mad would I become, had I dwelt afar, not knowing Him.
There's no worship in Mosque or Temple or on special holy day.
At every step I have my Mecca and Kāśi; sacred is every moment.

There are many similarities between the poems of the *Bāuls* and those of the North Indian mystics whom we discussed in the last chapter. However, the *Bāuls* are less organized and have not crystallized themselves into fixed orders. It is probable that they were influenced by the medieval mystics of North India, but simple *Bhakti* tradition is so deeply rooted in the soil, springing up in every age in different parts of the country, that it is really very difficult to trace the origin of these movements. There is some similarity between *Bāul* beliefs and those of some of the cults mentioned in the *Atharvaveda*, so that movements of this sort may well have appeared in India throughout her history.

The *Bāuls* learn their customs from their *gurus*, and in fact this is how their traditions are maintained. The *guru* passes on the lessons of the past to the *Bāuls* of the future. In their poetry they sometimes deny the existence of human *gurus*, using the term metaphorically to refer to whatever makes them think of, or understand, God.

Would you make obeisance to your *guru*, O my heart?
He is there at every step, on all sides of the path,
For numberless are your *gurus*.
To how many of them would you make your obeisance?
The welcome offered to you is your *guru*, the agony inflicted on you is your *guru*,
Every wrench at your heartstrings that makes the tears to flow is your *guru*.

Sometimes the *Bāuls* call the *guru* '*śūnya*' (lit., nothing, emptiness). This does not imply an absence of *gurus* (for the same word has also been used to denote the Supreme), but their constant presence. In practice, however, the *Bāuls*, like most other Indian religious sects, show great regard for their *gurus*.

The *Bāuls* are not ascetics in the usual sense, nor do they believe in celibacy. Indeed they claim that earthly love helps them to feel the Divine love. This belief, like the ideas and practices of the *Tantras*, is a little dangerous, and reports of moral lapses have sometimes brought disrepute on the whole *Bāul* movement.

Another *Bāul* doctrine is *trikāla-yoga*, harmony between past, present, and future. By failing to give adequate weight to each dimension of time, this doctrine preaches, we may destroy the continuity of our life. 'Your life is an expensive bridge of marble, but, alas, it fails to connect both banks of the river.' The *Bāuls* also emphasize the necessity of harmony between material and spiritual needs.

But the *Bāuls* are less known for their doctrines than for their simple moving songs. In fact the essence of their movements has been side-stepping the scriptures and having a direct relation with God. A *Vaishṇava* once read out to a *Bāul* long sections from his scriptures showing that religious activities should be regulated according to these teachings. The *Bāul*'s characteristic reply, in the form of an impromptu song was:

A goldsmith, methinks, has come into the flower garden.
He will appraise the lotus
By rubbing it on his touchstone.

Whatever one's religious belief, it is difficult to deny the appeal of the poetry of the *Bāuls*, which is simple, sensitive, and direct. It is not surprising, therefore, that sophisticated poets like Rabindranath Tagore were vastly influenced by the works of these poets of the lowest strata of Indian society.

Ah, where am I to find Him, the Man of my heart?
Alas, since I lost Him, I wander in search of Him
Through lands near and far.[1]

1. This chapter has much in common with my article on the *Bāuls* in the *Visvabharati Quarterly*, reprinted as an Appendix in Rabindranath Tagore's *The Religion of Man*, London, 1931.

CHAPTER 20

Present Trends

IN the last two hundred years Hinduism has been greatly influenced by the impact of the West. It has not produced any really new doctrine, but it has presented its old thought in a new light. These new developments are partly the result of the influence of Christianity, but not entirely. Indian society has undergone considerable changes since the advent of the modern age, and it is only natural that this should result in certain changes of ideas. The development is also connected with the rise of a new middle class.

The first period of Western impact, which covers the eighteenth and early nineteenth centuries, is characterized by considerable conversion of Hindus to Christianity. Hindu religious leaders seem to have been at a loss in face of this challenge and little attempt was made to prevent conversion. However, this period did not last very long and in fact the number of conversions seems to have been fairly small in view of the heavy impact of the West on India. This does not, however, mean that Christianity had no effect, since in trying to prevent Hindus from becoming Christians the Hindu leaders were forced to carry out considerable reform of religious practices and to revive many of the old aspects of Hindu thought which had been forgotten in most branches of degenerate Hinduism.

This brings us to the second period, which has often been called the period of 'Hindu Revivalism' or 'Hindu Reformism' and was indeed a bit of both. The pioneer in this movement was Raja Rammohan Roy (1774–1833) – an altogether remarkable figure. He was a scholar – who knew Arabic, Persian, Hebrew, Greek, and Latin along with Sanskrit and his native Bengali – and he read the scriptures of most of the world's religions in the original, only to find that there was not much difference between them. In 1828 he founded the *Brāhmo Samāj*, based on the unitarian doctrines of the *Upanishads*. In doing this he had to face the opposition of orthodox Hindus, among whom some of the less sophisticated even claimed that the *Upanishads* had actually been written by Rammohan himself to strengthen his case. While in matters of religion Rammohan turned back to the *Upanishads* of the eighth century B.C., his outlook on social matters was progressive. He was very keen that the Indians should learn Western sciences, and wrote to the Governor General of India emphasizing the need for education in 'mathematics, natural philosophy, chemistry, anatomy, and other useful sciences'. It was his agitation for the abolition of the *satī*,[1] that led the British Government to act. He was connected with many newspapers, ran a Bengali-English magazine and a Persian weekly, and lead a campaign against the enactment of 1823 dealing with the control of the Press.

Rammohan's work was continued by Devendranath Tagore (1817–1905), a saintly character who did much to consolidate the Upanishadic faith of the *Brāhmo Samāj*. His son, the poet Rabindranath (1861–1941), although born a *Brāhmo*, saw that the *Sāmaj* had one great weakness: it embraced only the *élite* and was out of tune with popular religious strivings. In his poetry and other writings we find Rabindranath voicing the wisdom of the outcastes, and in his Hibbert Lectures (1930) at Oxford he expressed his love for the poetry of the medieval mystics and the *Bāuls*. Finally, there was also one branch of the *Brāhmo Samāj*, under the leadership of Keshab Chandra Sen (1834–84), which had a more Christian outlook.

Another Hindu revivalist movement was the *Ārya Samāj* founded in 1875 by Swami Dayanand Saraswati (1824–83). This school was rather revivalistic in its outlook, and its slogan was 'Back to the *Vedas*'. It did very good social work, attempting to spread education and to raise the

1. This criminal custom never had any proper scriptural sanction. It was mainly prevalent among the upper classes of certain sections of the Hindu population. Earlier, Akbar, the Great Moghul, had tried to stop it, and the Hindu *Mārāṭhā* kings were also opposed to it. But they had not succeeded in eradicating the evil.

standards of the backward classes. It had an enthusiastic following in the United Provinces and the Punjab, and it is perhaps alone among Hindu movements in believing in proselytization.

Another new school of Hinduism besides the *Brāhmo Samāj* developed in Bengal under the influence of Ramakrishna Paramahamsa (1834–86). Ramakrishna was in a direct line with the *Bhakti* movement and represented a tradition very different from that of the *Brāhmo* trend. His approach was not intellectual and he put much emphasis on simple devotion to God. He combined the trend of popular Hinduism, including its many images, with a belief in a lovable Almighty God, for, he said, he could see God in so many forms. This is of course in direct line with the *Vedānta*, but he himself cared little for the scriptures and preached pure *bhakti* without theological complications. His strange personality attracted many people, including Romain Rolland, who wrote a biography of him. His disciple, Swami Vivekananda (1862–1902), spread this Vedāntic doctrine of *Advaita* (non-dualism) in India and abroad, and many Western countries now have branches of the Ramakrishna Mission. In many ways Vivekananda's personality was very different from that of his master. He was intensely interested in social problems, declared himself a socialist, and wanted to 'make a European society with India's religion'. The Ramakrishna Mission has done very good social work, spreading education, providing medical treatment and relief for the needy, and making Hindu religious thought known in the West.

In the South, the most important figure of this kind was Ramana Maharshi (1879–1950), who taught no formal doctrine but gave expression to the doctrine of the *Ātman* in his religious discussions.

In this connexion we must mention also the name of Shri Aurobindo Ghose, who started a school of Hinduism on the teachings of the *Yoga*, and of course that of Mahatma Gandhi, who, through his teachings and example, made the teachings of the *Gītā* into a living faith for a large section of the people. It was Bal Gangadhar Tilak, a politician of late nineteenth and early twentieth century, who focused attention on the *Gītā*, and Mahatma Gandhi carried on the tradition. The *Bhagavad-Gītā* have always appealed to the man of action, just as the *Upanishads* have always held an appeal for the contemplative intellectual.

To sum up, it might be said that the impact of the West has produced *new* schools of thought which have emphasized *old* doctrines. This does not mean that nothing in Hinduism has changed, for Hinduism has shown many trends in the past and it is important and significant that some of them are today more popular than others.

I should not like to forecast the future. Hindus have always believed in the existence of many ways of reaching God. The form of the religion may change, but as a Hindu, I believe that the craving for the Supreme cannot die. I should like to close this chapter by quoting from the *Upanishads*.

> Ya eko varṇo bahudhā śaktyogāt
> Varṇān anekān nihitārtho dadhāti.
> Vicaiti cānte viśvamādau sa devah
> Sa no buddhyā śubhayā samyunaktu.
> (*Śvetāśvatara Upanishad*, IV, 1.)

He who is one, and who dispenses the inherent needs of all peoples and all times, who is in the beginning and the end of all things, may He unite us with the bond of Goodwill.

Part Three

EXTRACTS FROM HINDU SCRIPTURES

A. ṚIGVEDA

(*Composed in the second millennium* B.C.; *the bulk of it perhaps around 1,200* B.C.)

1. TO THE UNKNOWN GOD

(*Maṇḍala* X, Hymn 121)[1]

'In the beginning there arose the Golden Child (Hiraṇya-garbha); as soon as born, he alone was the lord of all that is. He stablished the earth and this heaven: – Who is the God to whom we shall offer sacrifice?

He who gives breath, he who gives strength, whose command all the bright gods revere, whose shadow is immortality, whose shadow is death: – Who is the God to whom we shall offer sacrifice?

He who through his might became the sole king of the breathing and twinkling world, who governs all this, man and beast: – Who is the God to whom we shall offer sacrifice?

He through whose might these snowy mountains are, and the sea, they say, with the distant river (the Rasa), he of whom these regions are indeed the two arms: – Who is the God to whom we shall offer sacrifice?

He through whom the awful heaven and the earth were made fast, he through whom the ether was stablished, and the firmament; he who measured the air in the sky: – Who is the God to whom we shall offer sacrifice?

He to whom heaven and earth, standing firm by his will, look up, trembling in their mind; he over whom the risen sun shines forth: – Who is the God to whom we shall offer sacrifice?

When the great waters went everywhere, holding the germ (Hiraṇya-garbha), and generating light, then there arose from them the (sole) breath of the gods: – Who is the God to whom we shall offer sacrifice?

He who by his might looked even over the waters which

1. Translation from *The Sacred Books of the East*, ed. Max Müller, Vol. XXXII.

held power (the germ) and generated the sacrifice (light), he who alone is God above all gods: – Who is the God to whom we shall offer sacrifice?

May he not hurt us, he who is the begetter of the earth, or he, the righteous, who begat the heaven; he who also begat the bright and mighty waters: – Who is the God to whom we shall offer sacrifice?

Prajāpati, no other than thou embraces all these created things. May that be ours which we desire when sacrificing to thee: may we be lords of wealth!

2. THE SONG OF CREATION

(*Maṇḍala* X, Hymn 129)[1]

Then was not non-existent nor existent: there was no realm of air, no sky beyond it.
What covered in, and where? and what gave shelter? Was water there, unfathomed depth of water?
Death was not then, nor was there aught immortal: no sign was there, the day's and night's divider.
That one thing, breathless, breathed by its own nature; apart from it was nothing whatsoever.
Darkness there was: at first concealed in darkness, this All was indiscriminated chaos.
All that existed then was void and formless: by the great power of Warmth was born that Unit.
Thereafter rose Desire in the beginning, Desire, the primal seed and germ of Spirit.
Sages who searched with their heart's thought discovered the existent's kinship in the non-existent.
Transversely was their severing line extended: what was above it then, and what below it?
There were begetters, there were mighty forces, free action here and energy up yonder.
Who verily knows and who can here declare it, when it was born and whence comes this creation?

1. Translation from *The Hymns of the Ṛigveda*, by R. T. H. Griffith, Vol. IV.

The gods are later than this world's production. Who knows, then, whence it first came into being?
He, the first origin of this creation, whether he formed it all or did not form it.
Whose eye controls this world in highest heaven, he verily knows it, or perhaps he knows not.

3. TO DAWN

(*Maṇḍala* I, Hymn 113)[1]

This light is come, amid all lights the fairest; born is the brilliant, far-extending brightness.
Night, sent away for Savitar's[2] uprising, hath yielded up a birthplace for the Morning.
The Fair, the Bright is come with her white offspring; to her the Dark One hath resigned her dwelling.
Akin, immortal, following each other, changing their colours, both the heavens move onward.
Common, unending is the Sisters' pathway; taught by the Gods, alternately they travel.
Fair-formed, of different hues and yet one-minded, Night and Dawn clash not, neither do they tarry.
Bright leader of glad sounds, our eyes behold her; splendid in hue she hath unclosed the portals.
She, stirring up the world, hath shown us riches; Dawn hath awakened every living creature.
Rich Dawn, she sets afoot the coiled-up sleeper, one for enjoyment, one for wealth or worship.
Those who saw little for extended vision. All living creatures hath the Dawn awakened.
One to high sway, one to exalted glory, one to pursue his gain and one his labour;
All to regard their different vocations, all moving creatures hath the Dawn awakened.

1. Translation from *The Hymns of the Ṛigveda*, by R. T. H. Griffith, Vol. I.

2. The Sun.

We see her there, the Child of Heaven, apparent, the young
Maid, flushing in her shining raiment.
Thou sovran lady of all earthly treasure, flush on us here,
auspicious Dawn, this morning.
She, first of endless morns to come hereafter, follows the path
of morns that have departed.
Dawn, at her rising, urges forth the living: him who is dead
she wakes not from his slumber.
As thou, Dawn, hast caused Agni to be kindled, and with
the Sun's eye hast revealed creation,
And hast awakened men to offer worship, thou hast performed, for Gods, a noble service.
How long a time, and they shall be together. – Dawns that
have shone and dawns to shine hereafter?
She yearns for former dawns with eager longing, and goes
forth gladly shining with the others.
Gone are the men who in the days before us looked on the
rising of the earlier Morning.
We, we the living, now behold her brightness, and they
come nigh who shall hereafter see her.
Foe-chaser, born of Law, the Law's protectress, joy-giver,
waker of all pleasant voices,
Auspicious, bringing food for gods' enjoyment, shine on us
here, most bright, O Dawn, this morning.
From days eternal hath Dawn shone, the Goddess, and
shows this light today, endowed with riches.
So will she shine on days to come; immortal she moves on in
her own strength, undecaying.
In the sky's borders hath she shone in splendour; the Goddess hath thrown off the veil of darkness.
Awakening the world with purple horses, on her well-harnessed chariot Dawn approaches.
Bringing all life-sustaining blessings with her, showing herself, she sheds forth brilliant lustre.
Last of the countless mornings that have vanished, first of
bright morns to come hath Dawn arisen.
Arise! the breath, the life, again hath reached us; darkness
hath passed away, and light approacheth.

She for the Sun hath left a path to travel; we have arrived where men prolong existence.
Singing the praises of refulgent Mornings, with his hymn's web, the priest, the poet, rises.
Shine then today, rich Maid, on him who lauds thee, shine down on us the gift of life and offspring.
Dawns giving sons all heroes, kine and horses, shining upon the man who brings oblations, –
These let the Soma-presser gain when ending his glad songs louder than the voice of Vāyu.
Mother of Gods, Aditi's form of glory, ensign of sacrifice, shine forth exalted.
Rise up, bestowing praise on our devotion; all-bounteous, make us chief among the people.
Whatever splendid wealth the Dawns brings with them to bless the man who offers praise and worship,
Even that may Mitra, Varuṇa vouchsafe us, and Aditi and Sindhu, Earth and Heaven.

4. TO RUDRA

(*Maṇḍala* VII, Hymn 46)[1]

Offer ye these songs to Rudra whose bow is strong, whose arrows are swift, the self-dependent god, the unconquered conqueror, the intelligent, whose weapons are sharp – may he hear us!

For, being the lord, he looks after what is born on earth; being the universal ruler, he looks after what is born in heaven. Protecting us, come to our protecting doors, be without illness among our people, O Rudra!

May that thunderbolt of thine, which, sent from heaven, traverses the earth, pass us by! A thousand medicines are thine, O thou who art freely accessible; do not hurt us in our kith and kin!

Do not strike us, O Rudra, do not forsake us! May we not be in thy way when thou rushest forth furiously. Let us have

1. Translation from *The Sacred Books of the East*, ed. Max Müller, Vol. XXXII.

our altar and a good report among men – protect us always with your favours!

5. TO FIRE

(*Maṇḍala* II, Hymn 4)[1]

I call for you Agni, shining with beautiful shine, praised with beautiful praise, the guest of the clans, the receiver of fine offerings, who is desirable like Mitra (or, like an ally), Jātavedas the god, among godly people.

The Bhṛigus worshipping him in the abode of the waters have verily established him among the clans of Āyu. Let him surpass all worlds, Agni, the steward of the gods, the possessor of quick horses.

The gods have established beloved Agni among the human clans as (people) going to settle (establish) Mitra. May he illuminate the nights that are longing (for him), he who should be treated kindly by the liberal (worshipper) in his house.

His prosperity is delightful as good pasture; delightful is his appearance when the burning one is driven forward, he who quickly shaking his tongue among the plants waves his tail mightily like a chariot-horse.

When they praised to me the monstrous might of the eater of the forests, he produced his (shining) colour as (he has done) for the Uśijs. With shining splendour he has shone joyously, he who having grown old has suddenly become young (again).

He who shines on the forests as if he were thirsty, who resounded like water on its path, like (the rattle of the wheels) of a chariot – he whose path is black, the hot, the joyous one has shone, laughing like the sky with its clouds.

He who has spread himself burning over the wide (earth), moves about like an animal, free, without a keeper. The flaming Agni, burning down the brushwood, with a black trail, has as it were, tasted the earth.

1. Translation from *The Sacred Books of the East*, ed. Max Müller, Vol. XLVI.

Now in the remembrance of thy former blessings this prayer has been recited to thee at the third sacrifice. Give to us, Agni, mighty strength with a succession of valiant men, with plenty of food; (give us) wealth with good progeny.

Give, O Agni, such vigour to thy praiser together with his liberal (lords), that the Gṛitsamadas, rich in valiant men, victorious over hostile plots, attaining (their aim) in secret, may overcome through thee (their rivals) who get behind.

B. ATHARVAVEDA

While the roots of the Atharvaveda *stretch to remote antiquity, it took its present form around 1,000* B.C.)

I. HYMN TO GODDESS EARTH

(Book XII, I, Verses 1–27)[1]

TRUTH, greatness, universal order (*ṛita*), strength, consecration, creative fervour (*tapas*), spiritual exaltation (*brahma*), the sacrifice, support the earth. May this earth, the mistress of that which was and shall be, prepare for us a broad domain!

The earth that has heights, and slopes, and great plains, that supports the plants of manifold virtue, free from the pressure that comes from the midst of men, she shall spread out for us, and fit herself for us!

The earth upon which the sea, and the rivers and the waters, upon which food and the tribes of men have arisen, upon which this breathing, moving life exists, shall afford us precedence in drinking!

The earth whose are the four regions of space, upon which food and the tribes of men have arisen, which supports the manifold breathing, moving things, shall afford us cattle and other possessions also!

The earth upon which of old the first men unfolded themselves, upon which the gods overcame the Asuras, shall procure for us (all) kinds of cattle, horses, and fowls, good fortune, and glory!

The earth that supports all, furnishes wealth, the foundation, the golden-breasted resting-place of all living creatures, she that supports Agni Vaiśvānara (the fire), and mates with Indra, the bull, shall furnish us with property!

The broad earth, which the sleepless gods ever attentively guard, shall milk for us precious honey, and, moreover, besprinkle us with glory!

1. Translation from *The Sacred Books of the East*, ed. Max Müller, Vol. XLII.

That earth which formerly was water upon the ocean (of space), which the wise (seers) found out by their skilful devices; whose heart is in the highest heaven, immortal, surrounded by truth, shall bestow upon us brilliancy and strength, (and place us) in supreme sovereignty!

That earth upon which the attendant waters jointly flow by day and night unceasingly, shall pour out milk for us in rich streams, and, moreover, besprinkle us with glory!

The earth which the Aśvins have measured, upon which Vishṇu has stepped out, which Indra, the lord of might, has made friendly to himself; she, the mother, shall pour forth milk for me, the son!

Thy snowy mountain heights, and thy forests, O earth, shall be kind to us! The brown, the black, the red, the multi-coloured, the firm earth, that is protected by Indra, I have settled upon, not suppressed, not slain, not wounded.

Into thy middle set us, O earth, and into thy navel, into the nourishing strength that has grown up from thy body; purify thyself for us! The earth is the mother, and I the son of the earth; Parjanya is the father; He, too, shall save us!

The earth upon which they (the priests) enclose the altar (vedi), upon which they, devoted to all (holy) works, unfold the sacrifice, upon which are set up, in front of the sacrifice, the sacrificial posts, erect and brilliant, that earth shall prosper us, herself prospering!

Him that hates us, O earth, him that battles against us, him that is hostile towards us with his mind and his weapons, do thou subject to us, anticipating (our wish) by deed!

The mortals born of thee live on thee, thou supportest both bipeds and quadrupeds. Thine, O earth, are these five races of men, the mortals, upon whom the rising sun sheds undying light with his rays.

These creatures all together shall yield milk for us; do thou, O earth, give us the honey of speech!

Upon the firm, broad earth, the all-begetting mother of the plants, that is supported by (divine) law, upon her, propitious and kind, may we ever pass our lives!

A great gathering-place thou, great (earth), hast become; great haste, commotion, and agitation are upon thee. Great Indra protects thee unceasingly. Do thou, O earth, cause us to brighten as if at the sight of gold: not any one shall hate us!

Agni (fire) is in the earth, in the plants, the waters hold Agni, Agni is in the stones; Agni is within men, Agnis (fires) are within cattle, within horses.

Agni glows from the sky, to Agni, the god, belongs the broad air. The mortals kindle Agni, the bearer of oblations that loveth thee.

The earth, clothed in Agni, with dark knees, shall make me brilliant and alert!

Upon the earth men give to the gods the sacrifice, the prepared oblation; upon the earth mortal men live pleasantly by food. May this earth give us breath and life, may she cause me to reach old age!

The fragrance, O earth, that has arisen upon thee, which the plants and the waters hold, which the Gandharvas and the Apsaras have partaken of, with that make me fragrant: not any one shall hate us!

That fragrance of thine which has entered into the lotus, that fragrance, O earth, which the immortals of yore gathered up at the marriage of Sūryā, with that make me fragrant: not any one shall hate us!

That fragrance of thine which is in men, the loveliness and charm that is in male and female, that which is in steads and heroes, that which is in the wild animals with trunks (elephants), the lustre that is in the maiden, O earth, with that do thou blend us: not any one shall hate us!

Rock, stone, dust is this earth; this earth is supported, held together. To this golden-breasted earth I have rendered obeisance.

The earth, upon whom the forest-sprung trees ever stand firm, the all-nourishing, compact earth, do we invoke.

2. PRAYER FOR EXEMPTION FROM THE DANGERS OF DEATH

(Book VIII, I)[1]

To the 'Ender', to Death be reverence! May thy in-breathing and thy out-breathing remain here! United here with (life's) spirit this man shall be, sharing in the sun, in the world of immortality (*amṛita*)!

Bhaga has raised him up, Soma with his rays (has raised) him up, the Maruts, the gods, (have raised) him up, Indra and Agni (have raised) him up unto well-being.

Here (shall be) thy (life's) spirit, here thy in-breathing, here thy life, here thy mind! We rescue thee from the toils of Nirṛiti (destruction) by means of our divine utterance.

Rise up hence, O man! Casting off the foot-shackles of death, do not sink down! Be not cut off from this world, from the sight of Agni and the sun!

The wind, Mātariśvan, shall blow for thee, the waters shall shower *amṛita* (ambrosia) upon thee, the sun shall shine kindly for thy body! Death shall pity thee: do not waste away!

Thou shalt ascend and not descend, O man! Life and alertness do I prepare for thee. Mount, forsooth, this imperishable, pleasant car; then in old age thou shalt hold converse with thy family!

Thy mind shall not go thither, shall not disappear! Do not become heedless of the living, do not follow the Fathers! All the gods shall preserve thee here!

Do not long after the departed, who conduct (men) afar! Ascend from the darkness, come to the light! We lay hold of thy hands.

The two dogs of Yama, the blake and the brindled one, that guard the road (to heaven), that have been dispatched, shall not (go after) thee! Come hither, do not long to be away; do not tarry here with thy mind turned to a distance!

Do not follow this path: it is terrible! I speak of that by

1. Translation from *The Sacred Books of the East*, ed. Max Müller, Vol. XLII.

which thou hast not hitherto gone. Darkness is this, O man, do not enter it! Danger is beyond, security here for thee.

May the fires that are within the waters guard thee, may (the fire) which men kindle guard thee, may Jātavedas Vaiśvānara (the fire common to all men) guard thee! Let not the heavenly (fire) together with the lightning burn thee!

Let not the flesh-devouring (fire) menace thee: move afar from the funeral pyre! Heaven shall guard thee, the earth shall guard thee, the sun and moon shall guard thee, the atmosphere shall guard thee against the divine missile!

May the alert and the watchful divinities guard thee, may he that sleeps not and nods not guard thee, may he that protects and is vigilant guard thee!

They shall guard thee, they shall protect thee. Reverence be to them. Hail be to them!

Into converse with the living Vāyu, Indra, Dhātar, and saving Savitar shall put thee; breath and strength shall not leave thee! Thy (life's) spirit do we call back to thee.

Convulsions that draw the jaws together, darkness, shall not come upon thee, nor (the demon) that tears out the tongue! How shalt thou then waste away? The Ādityas and Vasus, Indra and Agni shall raise thee up unto well-being!

The heavens, the earth, Prajāpati, have rescued thee. The plants with Soma their king have delivered thee from death.

Let this man remain right here, ye gods, let him not depart hence to yonder world! We rescue him from death with (a charm) a thousandfold strength.

I have delivered thee from death. The (powers) that furnish strength shall breathe upon thee. The (mourning women) with dishevelled hair, they that wail lugubriously, shall not wail over thee!

I have snatched thee (from death), I have obtained thee; thou hast returned with renewed youth. O thou, that art (now) sound of limb, for thee sound sight and sound life have I obtained.

It has shone upon thee, light has arisen, darkness has departed from thee. We remove from thee death, destruction, and disease.

C. UPANISHADS

(*The* Upanishads *were composed over a very long period, but the bulk of them were produced around 800 or 700* B.C.)

1. ĪŚA UPANISHAD[1]

ALL this, whatsoever moves on earth, is to be hidden in the Lord (the Self). When thou hast surrendered all this, then thou mayest enjoy. Do not covet the wealth of any man!

Though a man may wish to live a hundred years, performing works, it will be thus with him; but not in any other way: work will thus not cling to a man.

There are the worlds of the Asuras covered with blind darkness. Those who have destroyed their self (who perform works, without having arrived at a knowledge of the true Self), go after death to those worlds.

That one (the Self), though never stirring, is swifter than thought. The Devas (senses) never reached it, it walked before them. Though standing still, it overtakes the others who are running. Mātariśvan (the wind, the moving spirit) bestows powers on it.

It stirs and it stirs not; it is far, and likewise near. It is inside of all this, and it is outside of all this.

And he who beholds all beings in the Self, and the Self in all beings, he never turns away from it.

When to a man who understands, the Self has become all things, what sorrow, what trouble can there be to him who once beheld that unity?

He (the Self) encircled all, bright, incorporeal, scatheless, without muscles, pure, untouched by evil; a seer, wise, omnipresent, self-existent, he disposed all things rightly for eternal years.

All who worship what is not real knowledge (good works),

1. Translation from *The Sacred Books of the East*, ed. Max Müller, Vol. I.

enter into blind darkness: those who delight in real knowledge, enter, as it were, into greater darkness.

One thing, they say, is obtained from real knowledge; another, they say, from what is not knowledge. Thus we have heard from the wise who taught us this.

He who knows at the same time both knowledge and not-knowledge, overcomes death through not-knowledge, and obtains immortality through knowledge.

All who worship what is not the true cause, enter into blind darkness: those who delight in the true cause, enter, as it were, into greater darkness.

One thing, they say, is obtained from (knowledge of) the cause; another, they say, from (knowledge of) what is not the cause. Thus we have heard from the wise who taught us this.

He who knows at the same time both the cause and the destruction (the perishable body), overcomes death by destruction (the perishable body), and obtains immortality through (knowledge of) the true cause.

The door of the True is covered with a golden disk. Open that, O Pūshan, that we may see the nature of the True.

O Pūshan, only seer, Yama (judge), Sūrya (sun), son of Prajāpati, spread thy rays and gather them! The light which is thy fairest form, I see it. I am what He is (viz. the person in the sun).

Breath to air, and to the immortal! Then this my body ends in ashes. Om! Mind, remember! Remember thy deeds! Mind, remember! Remember thy deeds!

Agni, lead us on to wealth (beatitude) by a good path, thou, O God, who knowest all things! Keep far from us crooked evil, and we shall offer thee the fullest praise! (Rv. I, 189, I).

2. BṚIHADĀRAṆYAKA UPANISHAD

(II Adhāya, 4 Brāhmaṇa)[1]

Now when Yājñavalkya was going to enter upon another state, he said: 'Maitreyī, verily I am going away from this my house (into the forest). Forsooth, let me make a settlement between thee and that Kātyāyanī (my other wife).'

Maitreyī said: 'My Lord, if this whole earth, full of wealth, belonged to me, tell me, should I be immortal by it?'

'No,' replied Yājñavalkya: 'like the life of rich people will be thy life. But there is no hope of immortality by wealth.'

And Maitreyī said: 'What should I do with that by which I do not become immortal? What my Lord knoweth (of immortality), tell that to me.'

Yājñavalkya replied: 'Thou who art truly dear to me, thou speakest dear words. Come, sit down, I will explain it to thee, and mark well what I say.'

And he said: 'Verily, a husband is not dear, that you may love the husband; but that you may love the Self, therefore a husband is dear.

'Verily, a wife is not dear, that you may love the wife; but that you may love the Self, therefore a wife is dear.

'Verily, sons are not dear, that you may love the sons; but that you may love the Self, therefore sons are dear.

'Verily, wealth is not dear, that you may love wealth; but that you may love the Self, therefore wealth is dear.

'Verily, the Brahman-class is not dear, that you may love the Brahman-class; but that you may love the Self, therefore the Brahman-class is dear.

'Verily, the Kshatra-class is not dear, that you may love the Kshatra-class; but that you may love the Self, therefore the Kshatra-class is dear.

'Verily the worlds are not dear, that you may love the worlds; but that you may love the Self, therefore the worlds are dear.

1. Translation from *The Sacred Books of the East*, ed. Max Müller, Vol. XV.

'Verily, the Devas are not dear, that you may love the Devas; but that you may love the Self, therefore the Devas are dear.

'Verily, creatures are not dear, that you may love the creatures; but that you may love the Self, therefore are creatures dear.

'Verily, everything is not dear that you may love everything; but that you may love the Self, therefore everything is dear.

'Verily, the Self is to be seen, to be heard, to be perceived, to be marked, O Maitreyī! When we see, hear, perceive, and know the Self, then all this is known.

'Whosoever looks for the Brahman-class elsewhere than in the Self, was abandoned by the Brahman-class. Whosoever looks for the Kshatra-class elsewhere than in the Self, was abandoned by the Kshatra-class. Whosoever looks for the worlds elsewhere than in the Self, was abandoned by the worlds. Whosoever looks for the Devas elsewhere than in the Self, was abandoned by the Devas. Whosoever looks for creatures elsewhere than in the Self, was abandoned by creatures. Whosoever looks for anything elsewhere than in the Self, was abandoned by everything. This Brahman-class, this Kshatra-class, these worlds, these Devas, these creatures, this everything, all is that Self.

'Now as the sounds of a drum, when beaten, cannot be seized externally (by themselves), but the sound is seized, when the drum is seized or the beater of the drum;

'And as the sounds of a conch-shell, when blown, cannot be seized externally (by themselves), but the sound is seized, when the shell is seized or the blower of the shell;

'And as the sounds of a lute, when played, cannot be seized externally (by themselves), but the sound is seized, when the lute is seized or the player of the lute;

'As the clouds of smoke proceed by themselves out of a lighted fire kindled with damp fuel, thus, verily, O Maitreyī, has been breathed forth from this great Being what we have as Ṛig-veda, Yajur-veda, Sāma-veda, Atharvāṅgirasas, Itihāsa (legends), Purāṇa (cosmogonies), Vidyā (knowledge), the Upanishads, Ślokas (verses), Sūtras (prose rules),

Anuvyākhyānas (glosses), Vyākhyānas (commentaries). From him alone all these were breathed forth.

'As all waters find their centre in the sea, all touches in the skin, all tastes in the tongue, all smells in the nose, all colours in the eye, all sounds in the ear, all percepts in the mind, all knowledge in the heart, all actions in the hands, all movements in the feet, and all the Vedas in speech, –

'As a lump of salt, when thrown into water, becomes dissolved into water, and could not be taken out again, but wherever we taste (the water) it is salt, – thus verily, O Maitreyī, does this great Being, endless, unlimited, consisting of nothing but knowledge, rise from out these elements, and vanish again in them. When he has departed, there is no more knowledge (name), I say, O Maitreyī.' Thus spoke Yājñavalkya.

Then Maitreyī said: 'Here thou hast bewildered me, Sir, when thou sayest that having departed, there is no more knowledge.'

But Yājñavalka replied: 'O Maitreyī, I say nothing that is bewildering. This is enough, O beloved, for wisdom.

'For when there is as it were duality, then one sees the other, one smells the other, one hears the other, one salutes the other, one perceives the other, one knows the other; but when the Self only is all this, how should he smell another, how should he see another, how should he hear another, how should he salute another, how should be perceive another, how should he know another? How should he know Him by whom he knows all this? How, O beloved, should he know (himself), the Knower?'

3. BṚIHADĀRAṆYAKA UPANISHAD

(III Adhyāya, 8 Brāhmaṇa)[1]

Then Vācaknavī said: 'Venerable Brāhmaṇas, I shall ask him two questions. If he will answer them, none of you, I think, will defeat him in any argument concerning Brahman.'

1. Translation from *The Sacred Books of the East*, ed. Max Müller, Vol. XV.

Yājñavalkya said: 'Ask, O Gārgī.'

She said: 'O Yājñavalkya, as the son of a warrior from the Kāśīs or Videhas might string his loosened bow, take two pointed, foe-piercing arrows in his hand and rise to do battle, I have risen to fight thee with two questions. Answer me these questions.'

Yājñavalkya said: 'Ask, O Gārgī.'

She said: 'O Yājñavalkya, that of which they say that it is above the heavens, beneath the earth, embracing heaven and earth, past, present, and future, tell me in what is it woven, like warp and woof?'

Yājñavalkya said: 'That of which they say that it is above the heavens, beneath the earth, embracing heaven and earth, past, present, and future, that is woven, like warp and woof, in the ether (*ākāśa*).'

She said: 'I bow to thee, O Yājñavalkya, who has solved me that question. Get thee ready for the second.'

Yājñavalkya said: 'Ask, O Gārgī.'

She said: 'O Yājñavalkya, that of which they say that it is above the heavens, beneath the earth, embracing heaven and earth, past, present, and future, tell me in what is it woven, like warp and woof?'

Yājñavalkya said: 'That of which they say that it is above the heavens, beneath the earth, embracing heaven and earth, past, present, and future, that is woven, like warp and woof, in the ether.'

Gārgī said: 'In what then is the ether woven, like warp and woof?'

He said: 'O Gārgī, the Brāhmaṇas call this the Akshara (the imperishable). It is neither coarse nor fine, neither short nor long, neither red (like fire) nor fluid (like water); it is without shadow, without darkness, without air, without ether, without attachment, without taste, without smell, without eyes, without ears, without speech, without mind, without light (vigour), without breath, without a mouth (or door), without measure, having no within and no without, it devours nothing, and no one devours it.

'By the command of that Akshara (the imperishable), O Gārgī, sun and moon stand apart. By the command of that Akshara, O Gārgī, heaven and earth stand apart. By the command of that Akshara, O Gārgī, what are called moments (*nimesha*), hours (*muhūrta*), days and nights, half-months, months, seasons, years, all stand apart. By the command of that Akshara, O Gārgī, some rivers flow to the East from the white mountains, others to the West, or to any other quarter. By the command of the Akshara, O Gārgī, men praise those who give, the gods follow the sacrificer, the fathers the Darvī-offering.

'Whosoever, O Gārgī, without knowing that Ahskara (the imperishable), offers oblations in this world, sacrifices, and performs penance for a thousand years, his work will have an end. Whosoever, O Gārgī, without knowing this Akshara, departs this world, he is miserable (like a slave). But he, O Gārgī, who departs this world, knowing this Akshara, he is a Brāhmaṇa.'

'That Brahman, O Gārgī, is unseen, but seeing; unheard, but hearing; unperceived, but perceiving; unknown, but knowing. There is nothing that sees but it, nothing that hears but it, nothing that perceives but it, nothing that knows but it. In that Akshara then, O Gārgī, the ether is woven, like warp and woof.'

Then said Gārgī: 'Venerable Brahmins, you may consider it a great thing, if you get off by bowing before him. No one, I believe, will defeat him in any argument concerning Brahman.' After that Vācaknavī held her peace.

4. CHĀNDOGYA UPANISHAD

(VI Prapāthaka)[1]

First Khaṇḍa

Harih, Om. There lived once Śvetaketu Āruṇeya (the grandson of Aruṇa). To him his father (Uddālaka, the son of Aruṇa) said: 'Śvetaketu, go to school; for there is none belonging to our race, darling, who, not having studied (the Veda), is, as it were, a Brahmin by birth only.'

1. Translation from *The Sacred Books of the East*, ed. Max Müller, Vol. I.

Having begun his apprenticeship (with a teacher) when he was twelve years of age, Śvetaketu returned to his father; when he was twenty-four, having then studied all the Vedas, – conceited, considering himself well-read, and stern.

His father said to him: 'Śvetaketu, as you are so conceited, considering yourself so well-read, and so stern, my dear, have you ever asked for that instruction by which we hear what cannot be heard, by which we perceive what cannot be perceived, by which we know what cannot be known?'

'What is that instruction, Sir?' he asked.

The father replied: 'My dear, as by one clod of clay all that is made of clay is known, the difference being only a name, arising from speech, but the truth being that all is clay;

'And as, my dear, by one nugget of gold all that is made of gold is known, the difference being only a name, arising from speech, but the truth being that all is gold;

'And as, my dear, by one pair of nail-scissors all that is made of iron (*kārshṇāyasam*) is known, the difference being only a name, arising from speech, but the truth being that all is iron, – thus, my dear, is that instruction.'

The son said: 'Surely, those venerable men (my teachers) did not know that. For if they had known it, why should they not have told it me? Do you, Sir, therefore tell me that.' 'Be it so,' said the father.

Second Khaṇḍa

'In the beginning, my dear, there was that only which is, one only, without a second. Others say, in the beginning there was that only which is not, one only, without a second; and from that which is not, that which is was born.

'But how could it be thus, my dear?' the father continued. 'How could that which is, be born of that which is not? No, my dear, only that which is, was in the beginning, one only, without a second.

'It thought, may I be many, may I grow forth. It sent forth fire.

'That fire thought, may I be many, may I grow forth. It sent forth water.

'And therefore whenever anybody anywhere is hot and perspires, water is produced on him from fire alone.

'Water thought, may I be many, may I grow forth. It sent forth earth (food).

'Therefore whenever it rains anywhere, most food is then produced. From water alone is eatable food produced.

Third Khaṇḍa

'Of all living things there are indeed three origins only, that which springs from an egg (oviparous), that which springs from a living being (viviparous), and that which springs from a germ.

'That Being (i.e. that which had produced fire, water, and earth) thought, let me now enter those three beings (fire, water, earth) with this liivng Self (*jīva ātmā*), and let me then reveal (develop) names and forms.

'Then that Being having said, Let me make each of these three tripartite (so that fire, water, and earth should each have itself for its principal ingredient, besides an admixture of the other two) entered into those three beings (*devatā*) with this living self only, and revealed names and forms.

'He made each of these tripartite; and how these three beings become each of them tripartite, that learn from me now, my friend!

Fourth Khaṇḍa

'The red colour of burning fire (*agni*) is the colour of fire, the white colour of fire is the colour of water, the black colour of fire the colour of earth. Thus vanishes what we call fire, as a mere variety, being a name, arising from speech. What is true (*satya*) are the three colours or forms).

'The red colour of the sun (*āditya*) is the colour of fire, the white of water, the black of earth. Thus vanishes what we call the sun, as a mere variety, being a name, arising from speech. What is true are the three colours.

'The red colour of the moon is the colour of fire, the

white of water, the black of earth. Thus vanishes what we call the moon, as a mere variety, being a name, arising from speech. What is true are the three colours.

'The red colour of the lightning is the colour of fire, the white of water, the black of earth. Thus vanishes what we call the lightning, as a mere variety, being a name, arising from speech. What is true are the three colours.

'Great householders and great theologians of olden times who knew this, have declared the same, saying, "No one can henceforth mention to us anything which we have not heard, perceived, or known." Out of these (three colours or forms) they knew all.

'Whatever they thought looked red, they knew was the colour of fire. Whatever they thought looked white, they knew was the colour of water. Whatever they thought looked black, they knew was the colour of earth.

'Whatever they thought was altogether unknown, they knew was some combination of those three beings (*devatā*).

'Now learn from me, my friend, how those three beings, when they reach man, become each of them tripartite.

Fifth Khaṇḍa

'The earth (food) when eaten becomes threefold; its grossest portion becomes faeces, its middle portion flesh, its subtilest portion mind.

'Water when drunk becomes threefold; its grossest portion becomes water, its middle portion blood, its subtilest portion breath.

'Fire (i.e. in oil, butter, etc.) when eaten becomes threefold; its grossest portion becomes bone, its middle portion marrow, its subtilest portion speech.

'For truly, my child, mind comes of earth, breath of water, speech of fire.'

'Please, Sir, inform me still more,' said the son.

'Be it so, my child,' the father replied.

Sixth Khaṇḍa

'That which is the subtile portion of curds, when churned, rises upwards, and becomes butter.

'In the same manner, my child, the subtile portion of earth (food), when eaten, rises upwards, and becomes mind.

'That which is the subtile portion of water, when drunk, rises upwards, and becomes breath.

'That which is the subtile portion of fire, when consumed, rises upwards, and becomes speech.

'For mind, my child, comes of earth, breath of water, speech of fire.'

'Please, Sir, inform me still more,' said the son.

'Be it so, my child,' the father replied.

Seventh Khaṇḍa

'Man (*purusha*), my son, consists of sixteen parts. Abstain from food for fifteen days, but drink as much water as you like, for breath comes from water, and will not be cut off, if you drink water.'

Śvetaketu abstained from food for fifteen days. Then he came to his father and said: 'What shall I say?' The father said: 'Repeat the Ṛik, Yajur, and Sāman verses.' He replied: 'They do not occur to me, Sir.'

The father said to him: 'As of a great lighted fire one coal only of the size of a firefly may be left, which would not burn much more than this (i.e. very little), thus, my dear son, one part only of the sixteen parts (of you) is left, and therefore with that one part you do not remember the Vedas. Go and eat!

'Then wilt thou understand me.' Then Śvetaketu ate, and afterwards approached his father. And whatever his father asked him, he knew it all by heart. Then his father said to him:

'As of a great lighted fire one coal of the size of a firefly, if left, may be made to blaze up again by putting grass upon it, and will thus burn more than this.

'Thus, my dear son, there was one part of the sixteen parts left to you, and that, lighted up with food, burnt up, and by it you remember now the Veda.' After that, he understood what his father meant when he said: 'Mind, my son, comes from food, breath from water, speech from fire.' He understood what he said, yea, he understood it.

Eighth Khaṇḍa

Uddālaka Ārunī said to his son Śvetaketu: 'Learn from me the true nature of sleep (*svapna*). When a man sleeps here, then, my dear son, he becomes united with the True, he is gone to his own (Self). Therefore they say (*svapiti*) he sleeps, because he is gone (*apīta*) to his own (*sva*).

'As a bird when tied by a string flies first in every direction, and finding no rest anywhere, settled down at last on the very place where it is fastened, exactly in the same manner, my son, that mind (the *jīva*, or living Self in the mind, see VI, 3, 2), after flying in every direction, and finding no rest anywhere, settles down on breath; for indeed, my son, mind is fastened to breath.

'Learn from me, my son, what are hunger and thirst. When a man is thus to be hungry, water is carrying away (digests) what has been eaten by him. Therefore as they speak of a cow-leader (*go-nāya*), a horse-leader (*aśva-nāya*), a man-leader (*purusha-nāya*), so they call water (which digests food and causes hunger) food-leader (*aśa-nāya*). Thus (by food digested, etc.), my son, know this offshoot (the body) to be brought forth, for this (body) could not be without a root (cause).

'And where could its root be except in food (earth)? And in the same manner, my son, as food (earth) too is an offshoot, seek after its root, viz. water. And as water too is an offshoot, seek after its root, viz. fire. And as fire too is an offshoot, seek after its root, viz. the True. Yes, all these creatures, my son, have their root in the True, they dwell in the True, they rest in the True.

'When a man is thus said to be thirsty, fire carries away what has been drunk by him. Therefore as they speak of a cow-leader (*go-nāya*), of a horse-leader (*aśva-nāya*), of a man-leader (*purusha-nāya*), so they call fire *udanyā*, thirst, i.e. water-leader. Thus (by water digested, etc.), my son, know this offshoot (the body) to be brought forth: this (body) could not be without a root (cause).

'And where could its root be except in water? As water is an offshoot, seek after its root, viz. fire. As fire is an offshoot, seek after its root, viz. the True. Yes, all these creatures, O son, have their root in the True, they dwell in the True, they rest in the True.

'And how these three beings (*devatā*), fire, water, earth, O son, when they reach man become each of them tripartite, has been said before (VI, 4, 7). When a man departs from hence, his speech is merged in his mind, his mind in his breath, his breath in heat (fire), heat in the Highest Being.

'Now that which is that subtile essence (the root of all), in it all that exists has its self. It is the True. It is the Self, and thou, O Śvetaketu, art it.'

'Please, Sir, inform me still more,' said the son.

'Be it so, my child,' the father replied.

Ninth Khaṇḍa

'As the bees, my son, make honey by collecting the juices of distant trees, and reduce the juice into one form,

'And as these juices have no discrimination, so that they might say, I am the juice of this tree or that, in the same manner, my son, all these creatures, when they have become merged in the True (either in deep sleep or in death), know not that they are merged in the True.

'Whatever these creatures are here, whether a lion, or a wolf, or a boar, or a worm, or a midge, or a gnat, or a mosquito, that they become again and again.

'Now that which is that subtile essence, in it all that exists has its self. It is the True. It is the Self, and thou, O Śvetaketu, art it.'

'Please, Sir, inform me still more,' said the son.

'Be it so, my child,' the father replied.

Tenth Khaṇḍa

'These rivers my son, run, the eastern (like the Gangā) towards the east, the western (like the Sindhu) towards the west. They go from sea to sea (i.e. the clouds lift up the water from the sea to the sky, and send it back as rain to the sea). They become indeed sea. And as those rivers, when they are in the sea, do not know, I am this or that river,

'In the same manner, my son, all these creatures, when they have come back from the True, know not that they have come back from the True. Whatever these creatures are here, whether a lion, or a wolf, or a boar, or a worm, or a midge, or a gnat, or a mosquito, that they become again and again.

'That which is that subtile essence, in it all that exists has its self. It is the True. It is the Self, and thou, O Śvetaketu, art it.'

'Please, Sir, inform me still more,' said the son.

'Be it so, my child,' the father replied.

Eleventh Khaṇḍa

'If some one were to strike at the root of this large tree here, it would bleed, but live. If he were to strike at its stem, it would bleed, but live. If he were to strike at its top, it would bleed, but live. Pervaded by the living Self that tree stands firm, drinking in its nourishment and rejoicing;

'But if the life (the living Self) leaves one of its branches, that branch withers; if it leaves a second, that branch withers; if it leaves a third, that branch withers. If it leaves the whole tree, the whole tree withers. In exactly the same manner, my son, know this.' Thus he spoke:

'This (body) indeed withers and dies when the living Self has left it; the living Self dies not.

'That which is that subtile essence, in it all that exists has its self. It is the True. It is the Self, and thou, O Śvetaketu, art it.'

'Please, Sir, inform me still more,' said the son.

'Be it so, my child,' the father replied.

Twelfth Khaṇḍa

'Fetch me from thence a fruit of the Nyagrodha tree.'

'Here is one, Sir.'

'Break it.'

'It is broken, Sir.'

'What do you see there?'

'These seeds, almost infinitesimal.'

'Break one of them.'

'It is broken, Sir.'

'What do you see there?'

'Not anything, Sir.'

The father said: 'My son, that subtile essence which you do not perceive there, of that very essence this great Nyagrodha tree exists.

'Believe it, my son. That which is the subtile essence, in it all that exists has its self. It is the True. It is the Self, and thou, O Śvetaketu, art it.'

'Please, Sir, inform me still more,' said the son.

'Be it so, my child,' the father replied.

Thirteenth Khaṇḍa

'Place this salt in water, and then wait on me in the morning.'

The son did as he was commanded.

The father said to him: 'Bring me the salt, which you placed in the water last night.'

The son having looked for it, found it not, for, of course, it was melted.

The father said: 'Taste it from the surface of the water. How is it?'

The son replied: 'It is salt.'

'Taste if from the middle. How is it?'

The son replied: 'It is salt.'

'Taste it from the bottom. How is it?'

The son replied: 'It is salt.'

The father said: 'Throw it away and then wait on me.'

He did so; but salt exists for ever.

Then the father said: 'Here also, is this body, forsooth, you do not perceive the True (*Sat*), my son; but there indeed it is.

'That which is the subtile essence, in it all that exists has its self. It is True. It is the Self, and thou, O Śvetaketu, art it.'

'Please, Sir, inform me still more,' said the son.

'Be it so, my child,' the father replied.

Fourteenth Khaṇḍa

'As one might lead a person with his eyes covered away from the Gandhāras, and leave him then in a place where there are no human beings; and as that person would turn towards the east, or the north, or the west, and shout, "I have been brought here with my eyes covered, I have been left here with my eyes covered."

'And as thereupon someone might loose his bandage and say to him "Go in that direction, it is Gandhāra, go in that direction," and as thereupon, having been informed and being able to judge for himself, he would by asking his way from village to village arrive at last in Gandhāra, – in exactly the same manner does a man, who meets with a teacher to inform him, obtain the true knowledge. For him there is only delay so long as he is not delivered (from the body); then he will be perfect.

'That which is that subtile essence, in it all that exists has its self. It is the True. It is the Self, and thou, O Śvetaketu, art it.'

'Please, Sir, inform me still more,' said the son.

'Be it so, my child,' the father replied.

Fifteenth Khaṇḍa

'If a man is ill, his relatives assemble round him and ask: "Dost thou know me? Dost thou know me?" Now as long as his speech is not merged in his mind, his mind in breath, breath in heat (fire), heat in the Highest Being (*devatā*), he knows them.

'But when his speech is merged in his mind, his mind in breath, breath in heat (fire), heat in the Highest Being, then he knows them not.

'That which is the subtile essence, in it all that exists has its self. It is the True. It is the Self, and thou, O Śvetaketu, art it.'

'Please, Sir, inform me still more,' said the son.

'Be it so, my child,' the father replied.

Sixteenth Khaṇḍa

'My child, they bring a man hither whom they have taken by the hand, and they say: "He has taken something, he has committed a theft." (When he denies they say) "Heat the hatchet for him." If he committed the theft, then he makes himself to be what he is not. Then the false-minded, having covered his true Self by a falsehood, grasps the heated hatchet – he is burnt, and he is killed.

'But if he did not commit the theft, then he makes himself to be what he is. Then the true-minded, having covered his true Self by truth, grasps the heated hatchet – he is not burnt, and he is delivered.

'As that (truthful) man is not burnt, thus has all that exists its self in That. It is the True. It is the Self, and thou, O Śvetaketu, art it.' He understood what he said, yea, he understood it.

5. MUṆḌAKA UPANISHAD

(III *Muṇḍaka*)[1]

First Khaṇḍa

Two birds, inseparable friends, cling to the same tree. One of them eats the sweet fruit, the other looks on without eating.

On the same tree man sits grieving, immersed, bewildered by his own impotence (*an-īśā*). But when he sees the other lord (*īśā*) contented and knows his glory, then his grief passes away.

When the seer sees the brilliant maker and lord (of the world) as the Person who has his source in Brahman, then he is wise, and shaking off good and evil, he reaches the highest oneness, free from passions;

For he is the Breath shining forth in all beings, and he who understands this becomes truly wise, not a talker only. He revels in the Self, he delights in the Self, and having performed his works (truthfulness, penance, meditation, etc.) he rests, firmly established in Brahman, the best of those who know Brahman.

By truthfulness, indeed, by penance, right knowledge, and abstinence must that Self be gained; the Self whom spotless anchorites gain is pure, and like a light within the body.

1. Translation from *The Sacred Books of the East*, ed. Max Müller, Vol. XV.

The true prevails, not the untrue; by the true the path is laid out, the way of the gods (*devayānah*), on which the old sages, satisfied in their desires, proceed to where there is that highest place of the True One.

That (true Brahman) shines forth grand, divine, inconceivable, smaller than small; it is far beyond what is far and yet near here, it is hidden in the cave (of the heart) among those who see it even here.

He is not apprehended by the eye, nor by speech, nor by the other senses, nor by penance or good works. When a man's nature has become purified by the serene light of knowledge, then he sees him, meditating on him as without parts.

That subtle Self is to be known by thought (*cetas*) there where breath has entered fivefold; for every thought of men is interwoven with the senses, and when thought is purified, then the Self arises.

Whatever state a man whose nature is purified imagines, and whatever desires he desires (for himself or for others), that state he conquers and those desires he obtains. Therefore let every man who desires happiness worship the man who knows the Self.

Second Khaṇḍa

He (the knower of the Self) knows that highest home of Brahman, in which all is contained and shines brightly. The wise who, without desiring happiness, worship that Person, transcend this seed (they are not born again.)

He who forms desires in his mind, is born again through his desires here and there. But to him whose desires are fulfilled and who is conscious of the true Self (within himself) all desires vanish, even here on earth.

That Self cannot be gained by the Veda, nor by understanding, nor by much learning. He whom the Self chooses, by him the Self can be gained. The Self chooses him (his body) as his own.

Nor is that Self to be gained by one who is destitute of strength, or without earnestness, or without right meditation. But if a wise man strives after it by those means (by strength, earnestness, and right meditation), then his Self enters the home of Brahman.

When they have reached him (the Self), the sages become satisfied through knowledge, they are conscious of their Self, their passions have passed away, and they are tranquil. The wise, having reached Him who is omnipresent everywhere devoted to the Self, enter into him wholly.

Having well ascertained the object of the knowledge of the Vedānta, and having purified their nature by the Yoka of renunciation, all anchorites, enjoying the highest immortality, become free at the time of the great end (death) in the worlds of Brahmā.

Their fifteen parts enter into their elements, their Devas (the senses) into their (corresponding) Devas. Their deeds and their Self with all his knowledge become all one in the highest Imperishable.

As the flowing rivers disappear in the sea, losing their name and their form, thus a wise man, freed from name and form, goes to the divine Person, who is greater than the great.

He who knows that highest Brahman, becomes even Brahman. In his race no one is born ignorant of Brahman. He overcomes grief, he overcomes evil; free from the fetters of the heart, he becomes immortal.

And this is declared by the following Ṛik-verse: 'Let a man tell this science of Brahman to those only who have performed all (necessary) acts, who are versed in the Vedas, and firmly established in (the lower) Brahman, who themselves offer as an oblation the one Ṛishi (Agni), full of faith, and by whom the rite of (carrying fire on) the head has been performed, (according to the rule of the Ātharvaṇas).'

The Ṛishi Aṅgiras formerly told this true (science); a man who has not performed the (proper) rites, does not read it. Adoration to the highest Ṛishis! Adoration to the highest Ṛishis!

D. BHAGAVAD-GĪTĀ[1]

(Composed mainly betweem 400 and 200 B.C. There are considerable differences of opinion about this dating as indeed about the dates of most of the early Hindu texts. Some consider the Bhagavad-gītā *to be pre-Buddhist, i.e., earlier than the sixth century B.C.)*

*

CHAPTER III

Arjuna said:

IF, O Janārdana! devotion is deemed by you to be superior to action, then why, O Keśava! do you prompt me to (this) fearful action? You seem, indeed, to confuse my mind by equivocal words. Therefore, declare one thing determinately, by which I may attain the highest good.

The Deity said:

O sinless one! I have already declared, that in this world there is a twofold path – that of the Sāṃkhyas by devotion in the shape of (true) knowledge; and that of the Yogins by devotion in the shape of action. A man does not attain freedom from action merely by not engaging in action; nor does he attain perfection by mere renunciation. For nobody ever remains even for an instant without performing some action; since the qualities of nature constrain everybody, not having free-will (in the matter), to some action. The deluded man who, restraining the organs of action, continues to think in his mind about objects of sense, is called a hypocrite. But he, O Arjuna! who restraining his senses by his mind, and being free from attachments, engages in devotion (in the shape) of action, with the organs of action, is far superior. Do you perform prescribed action, for action is better than inaction, and the support of your body, too, cannot be accomplished with inaction. This world is fettered by all action other than action for the purpose of the sacrifice. Therefore, O son of Kuntī! do you, fasting off

1. Translation from *The Sacred Books of the East*, ed. Max Müller, Vol. VIII.

attachment, perform action for that purpose. The Creator, having in olden times created men together with the sacrifice, said: 'Propagate with this. May it be the giver to you of the things you desire. Please the gods with this, and may those gods please you. Pleasing each other, you will attain the highest good. For pleased with the sacrifices, the gods will give you the enjoyments you desire. And he who enjoys himself without giving them what they have given, is, indeed, a thief.' The good, who eat the leavings of a sacrifice, are released from all sins. But the unrighteous ones, who prepare food for themselves only, incur sin. From food are born (all) creatures; from rain is the production of food; rain is produced by sacrifices; sacrifices are the result of action; know that action has its source in the Vedas; the Vedas come from the Indestructible. Therefore the all-comprehending Vedas are always concerned with sacrifices. He who in this world does not turn round the wheel revolving thus is of sinful life, indulging his senses, and O son of Pṛithā! he lives in vain. But the man who is attached to his self only, who is contented in his self, and is pleased with his self, has nothing to do. He has no interest at all in what is done, and none whatever in what is not done, in this world; nor is any interest of his dependent on any being. Therefore always perform action, which must be performed, without attachment. For a man, performing action without attachment, attains the Supreme. By action alone, did Janaka and the rest work for perfection. And having regard also to the keeping of people (to their duties) you should perform action. Whatever a great man does, that other men also do. And people follow whatever he receives as authority. There is nothing, O son of Pṛithā! for me to do in (all) the three worlds, nothing to acquire which has not been acquired. Still I do engage in action. For should I at any time not engage without sloth in action, men would follow in my path from all sides, O son of Pṛithā! If I did not perform actions, these worlds would be destroyed I should be the cause of caste-interminglings; and I should be ruining these people. As the ignorant act, O descendant of Bharata! with attachment to action, so should a wise man act without attachment, wishing to keep the people (to their duties). A wise man should not shake the convictions of the ignorant who are attached to actions, but acting with devotion (himself) should make them apply themselves to all action. He whose mind is deluded by egoism thinks himself the doer of the actions, which in every way, are done by the qualities of nature. But he, O you of mighty arms! who knows the truth about the difference from qualities and the difference from actions, forms no attachments, believing that qualities deal with qualities. But those who are deluded by the qualities of nature form attachments to the actions of the qualities. A man of perfect knowledge should not shake these men of imperfect knowledge (in their convictions). Dedicating all actions to me with a mind knowing the relation of the supreme and individual self, engage in battle without desire, without (any feeling that this or that is) mine, and without any mental trouble. Even those men who always act on this opinion of mine, full of faith, and without carping, are released from all actions. But those who carp at my opinion and do not act upon it, know them to be devoid of discrimination, deluded as regards all knowledge, and ruined. Even a man of knowledge acts consonantly to his own nature. All beings follow nature. What will restraint effect? Every sense has its affections and aversions towards its objects fixed. One should not become subject to them, for they are one's opponents. One's own duty, though defective, is better than another's duty well performed. Death in (performing) one's own duty is preferable; the (performance of the) duty of others is dangerous.

Arjuna said:

But by whom, O descendant of Vṛishṇi! is man impelled, even though unwilling, and, as it were, constrained by force, to commit sin?

The Deity said:

It is desire, it is wrath, born from the quality of passion; it is very ravenous, very sinful. Know that that is the foe in this world. As fire is enveloped by smoke, a mirror by dust, the foetus by the womb, so is this enveloped by desire. Knowledge, O son of Kuntī! is enveloped by this constant foe of the man of knowledge, in the shape of desire, which is like a fire and insatiable. The senses, the mind, and the understanding are said to be its seat; with these it deludes the embodied (self) after enveloping knowledge. Therefore, O chief of the descendants of Bharata! first restrain your senses, then cast off this sinful thing which destroys knowledge and experience. It has been said, Great are the senses, greater than the senses is the mind, greater than the mind is the understanding. What is greater than the understanding is that. Thus knowing that which is higher than the understanding, and restraining (your) self by (your) self, O you of mighty arms! destroy this unmanageable enemy in the shape of desire.

CHAPTER XII

Arjuna said:

Of the worshippers, who thus, constantly devoted, meditate on you, and those who (meditate) on the unperceived and indestructible, which best know devotion?

The Deity said:

Those who being constantly devoted, and possessed of the highest faith, worship me with a mind fixed on me, are deemed by me to be the most devoted. But those who, restraining the (whole) group of the senses, and with a mind at all times equable, meditate on the indescribable, indestructible, unperceived (principle) which is all-pervading, unthinkable, indifferent, immovable, and constant, they, intent on the good of all beings, necessarily attain to me. For those whose minds are attached to the unperceived, the trouble is much greater. Because the unperceived goal is obtained by embodied (beings) with difficulty. As to those, however, O son of Pṛithā! who, dedicating all their actions to me, and (holding) me as their highest (goal), worship me, meditating on me with a devotion towards none besides me, and whose minds are fixed on me, I, without delay, come forward as their deliverer from the ocean of this world of death. Place your mind on me only; fix your understanding on me. In me you will dwell hereafter, (there is) no doubt. But if you are unable to fix your mind steadily on me, then, O Dhanañjaya! endeavour to obtain me by the abstraction of mind (resulting) from continuous meditation. If you are unequal even to continuous meditation, then let acts for (propitiating) me be your highest (aim). Even performing actions for (propitiating) me, you will attain perfection. If you are unable to do even this, then resort to devotion to me, and, with self-restraint, abandon all fruit of action. For knowledge is better than continuous meditation; concentration is esteemed higher than knowledge; and the abandonment of fruit of action than concentration; from (that) abandonment, tranquillity soon (results). That devotee of mine, who hates no being, who is friendly and compassionate, who is free from egoism, and from (the idea that this is, that is) mine, to whom happiness and misery are alike, who is forgiving, contented, constantly devoted, self-restrained, and firm in his determinations, and whose mind and understanding are devoted to me, he is dear to me. He through whom the world is not agitated, and who is not agitated by the world, who is free from joy and anger and fear and agitation, he too is dear to me. That devotee of mine, who is unconcerned, pure, assiduous, impartial, free from distress, who abandons all actions (for fruit), he is dear to me. He who is full of devotion to me, who feels no joy and no aversion, who does not grieve and does not desire, who abandons (both what is) agreeable and (what is) disagreeable, he is dear to me. He who is alike to friend and foe, as also in honour and dishonour, who is alike in cold and heat, pleasure and pain, who is free from attachments, to whom praise and blame are alike, who is taciturn, and contented with anything whatever (that comes), who is homeless, and of a steady mind, and full of devotion, that man is dear to me. But those devotees who, imbued with faith, and (regarding) me as their highest (goal), resort to this holy (means for attaining) immortality, as stated, they are extremely dear to me.

CHAPTER XIII

The Deity said:

This body, O son of Kuntī! is called Kshetra, and the learned call him who knows it the Kshetrajña. And know me also, O descendant of Bharata! to be the Kshetrajña in all Kshetras. The knowledge of Kshetra and Kshetrajña is deemed by me (to be real) knowledge. Now hear from me in brief what that Kshetra (is), what (it is) like, what changes (it undergoes), and whence (it comes), and what is he, and what his powers, (all which) is sung in various ways by sages in numerous hymns, distinctly, and in well-settled texts full of argument, giving indications or full instruction about the Brahman. The great elements, egoism, the understanding, the unperceived also, the ten senses, and the one, and the five objects of sense, desire, aversion, pleasure, pain, body, consciousness, courage, this in brief has been declared the Kshetra with changes. Absence of vanity, absence of ostentatiousness, absence of hurtfulness, forgiveness, straightforwardness, devotion to a preceptor, purity, steadiness, self-restraint, indifference towards objects of sense, and also absence of egoism; perception of the misery and evil of birth, death, old age, and disease; absence of attachment, absence of self-identifying regard for son, wife, home, and so forth; and constant equability on the approach of (both what is) agreeable and (what is) disagreeable; unswerving devotion to me, without meditation on anyone else; resorting to clean places, distaste for assemblages of men, constancy in knowledge of the relation of the individual self to the supreme, perception of the object of knowledge of the truth, this is called knowledge; that is ignorance which is opposed to this I will declare that which is the object of knowledge, knowing which one reaches immortality; the highest Brahman, having no beginning nor end, which cannot be said to be existent or non-existent. It has hands and feet on all sides, it has eyes, heads, and faces on all sides, it has ears on all sides, it stands pervading everything in the world. Possessed of the qualities of all the senses, (but) devoid of all senses, unattached, it supports all, is devoid of qualities, and the enjoyer of qualities. It is within all things and without them; it is movable and also immovable; it is unknowable through (its) subtlety; it stands afar and near. Not different in (different) things, but standing as though different, it should be known to be supporter of (all) things, and that which absorbs and creates (them). It is the radiance even of the radiant (bodies); it is said (to be) beyond darkness. It is knowledge, the object of knowledge, that which is to be attained to by knowledge, and placed in the heart of all. Thus in brief have Kshetra, knowledge, and the object of knowledge been declared. My devotee, knowing this, becomes fit for assimilation with me. Know nature and spirit both (to be) without beginning, and know all developments and qualities (to be) produced from nature. Nature is said to be the origin of the capacity of working (residing) in the body and the senses; and spirit is said (to be) the origin of the capacity of enjoying pleasures and pains. For spirit with nature joined, enjoys the qualities born of nature. And the cause of its birth in good or evil wombs is the connexion with the qualities. The supreme spirit in this body is called supervisor, adviser, supporter, enjoyer, the great lord, and the supreme self also. He who thus knows nature and spirit, together with the qualities, is not born again, however living. Some by concentration see the self in the self by the self; others by the Śāṃkhya-yoga; and others still by the Karma-yoga; others yet, not knowing this, practise concentration, after hearing from others. They, too, being (thus) devoted to hearing (instruction) cross beyond death. Whatever thing movable or immovable comes into existence, know that to be from the connexion of Kshetra and Kshetrajña, O chief of the descendants of Bharata! He sees (truly) who sees the supreme lord abiding alike in all entities, and not destroyed though they are destroyed. For he who sees the lord abiding everywhere alike, does not destroy himself by himself, and then reaches the highest goal. He sees (truly), who sees (all) actions (to be) in every way done by nature alone, and likewise the self (to be) not the doer. When a man sees all the variety of entities as existing in one, and (all as) emanating from that, then he becomes (one with) the Brahman. This inexhaustible supreme self, being without beginning and without qualities, does not act, and is not tainted, O son of Kuntī! though stationed in the body. As by (reason of its) subtlety the all-pervading space is not tainted, so the self stationed in every body is not tainted. As the sun singly lights up all this world, so the Kshetrajña, O descendant of Bharata! lights up the whole Kshetra. Those who, with the eye of knowledge, thus understand the difference between Kshetra and Kshetrajña, and the destruction of the nature of all entities, go to the supreme.

Index